SALOME

Oscar Wilde

edited by Kimberly J. Stern

broadview editions

Library and Archives Canada Cataloguing in Publication

Wilde, Oscar, 1854-1900
[Salomé. English]
  Salome / Oscar Wilde ; edited by Kimberly J. Stern.

(Broadview editions)
This edition of the play uses the English translation by Wilde's lover,
  Lord Alfred Douglas, and overseen by Wilde himself.
Translation of: Salomé.
Includes bibliographical references.
ISBN 978-1-55481-189-2 (pbk.)

  1. Salome (Biblical figure)—Drama. 2. Tragedies. I. Stern, Kimberly Jo, 1977-, editor II. Title. III. Title: Salomé. English. IV. Series: Broadview editions

PR5820.S2E5 2015   822'.8   C2015-900181-1

Broadview Editions

The Broadview Editions series represents the ever-changing canon of literature in English by bringing together texts long regarded as classics with valuable lesser-known works.

Advisory editor for this volume: Michel Pharand

Broadview Press is an independent, international publishing house, incorporated in 1985.

We welcome comments and suggestions regarding any aspect of our publications— please feel free to contact us at the addresses below or at broadview@broadviewpress.com.

North America
PO Box 1243, Peterborough, Ontario K9J 7H5, Canada
555 Riverwalk Parkway, Tonawanda, NY 14150, USA
Tel: (705) 743-8990; Fax: (705) 743-8353
email: customerservice@broadviewpress.com

UK, Europe, Central Asia, Middle East, Africa, India, and Southeast Asia
Eurospan Group, 3 Henrietta St., London WC2E 8LU, United Kingdom
Tel: 44 (0) 1767 604972; Fax: 44 (0) 1767 601640
email: eurospan@turpin-distribution.com

Australia and New Zealand
Footprint Books
1/6a Prosperity Parade, Warriewood, NSW 2102, Australia
Tel: 61 1300 260 090; Fax: 61 02 9997 3185
email: info@footprint.com.au

www.broadviewpress.com

Broadview Press acknowledges the financial support of the Government of Canada through the Canada Book Fund for our publishing activities.

Typesetting and assembly: True to Type Inc., Claremont, Canada.

PRINTED IN CANADA

Contents

SALOME

broadview editions
series editor: L.W. Conolly

Acknowledgements

Given the wide range of sources, languages, and historical documents needed to contextualize a drama such as *Salome*, the research for this volume has been an enormous undertaking. These efforts would not have come to fruition without the assistance of the Rosenbach Library and Museum (Philadelphia, PA) and of Elizabeth E. Fuller in particular. I am also deeply indebted to the library support staff at Longwood University, as well as my colleagues E. Derek Taylor (for his generous and insightful reading of early drafts) and Wade Edwards (for his invaluable assistance with the French language sources). I would additionally like to thank the editors and publication team at Broadview Press—in particular series editor Leonard Conolly—for giving such rigorous attention to the manuscript and helping to preserve the complexity of this work in its entirety.

I am enormously grateful to those individuals, publishers, and institutions who have granted permission for the reprinting of materials included within this edition. The excerpt from Stéphane Mallarmé's "Hérodiade" (Appendix A6) is reprinted by permission of Peter Manson and Miami UP from *Stéphane Mallarmé, The Poems in Verse*, translation and notes by Peter Manson (Miami UP, 2012). Gustave Moreau's "L'Apparition" (Appendix B1) is reproduced courtesy of the Musée d'Orsay (Paris), the Réunion des Musées Nationaux, and Art Resource. A selection from Charles Ricketts's *Self-Portrait* (Appendix E1) is reprinted by permission of Leonie Sturge-Moore and Charmian O'Neil. The photograph of Sarah Bernhardt in costume as Salome (Appendix E3) appears courtesy of the New York Public Library. The "plan de la scene" by Oscar Wilde (Appendix E9) appears courtesy of the Rosenbach Museum and Library, Philadelphia. The photograph of Alice Guszalewicz in costume as Salome (Appendix E13) is provided by Bridgeman Art Library Limited (Bridgeman Images).

Introduction

Although Oscar Wilde is most widely known for his society plays (*Lady Windermere's Fan, A Woman of No Importance, An Ideal Husband,* and *The Importance of Being Earnest*), it is *Salome* that he singled out as his most daring literary achievement. In June 1897, writing from Reading Gaol, Wilde reflected: "If I were asked of myself as a dramatist, I would say that my unique position was that I had taken the Drama, the most objective form known to art, and made it as personal a mode of expression as the Lyric or the Sonnet, while enriching the characterization of the stage, and enlarging—at any rate in the case of *Salomé*—its artistic horizon."[1] *Salome* is in many ways unlike anything else Wilde wrote. It has been described as a "horror play," "a masterpiece in sadism," or, in the words of an oft-quoted 1893 review for *The Times*, "an arrangement in blood and ferocity, morbid, *bizarre,* repulsive."[2] Where Wilde saw the expansion of artistic horizons, others it would seem saw an unfamiliar and potentially treacherous landscape. Yet this initial skepticism, culminating in the play's suppression from the English stage during Wilde's lifetime, only highlights the bold and innovative aesthetic he sought to capture in *Salome.*

As the following pages will demonstrate, the genesis, distribution, and performance history of *Salome* reveal a striking record of border-crossing. It is a play written in French by an Irish author and only later translated into English. It was banned for nearly fifty years in England and yet became the impetus for countless adaptations around the world. Wilde drew on a motley source base for his play (including Scripture, Renaissance painting, and French symbolist poetry), yet synthesized these sources into a wholly original and cohesive one-act drama. On nearly every page, *Salome* appeals to the senses, and yet its attention to vision, texture, and movement is precisely what justifies its classification as a work of philosophical substance. In short, *Salome* eludes any one system of aesthetic, cultural, or intellectual classification. It was in this spirit that Max Beerbohm described the play as "so modern that its publication in any century would seem premature" (Appendix C5, p. 116). For the modern reader,

---

1   Oscar Wilde, *The Complete Letters of Oscar Wilde,* ed. Merlin Holland and Rupert Hart-Davis (New York: Henry Holt and Company, 2000), 874.
2   Lewis Broad, *The Friendships and Follies of Oscar Wilde* (London: Hutchinson, 1954), 104, 105; Appendix C6, p. 117.

Salome thus exemplifies the very real ways in which Wilde reflected the spirit of his own time—a time when genres, languages, identities, and cultures were subject to collision and reinterpretation.

The Secular and the Divine

In the New Testament, Salome appears for only a few lines. On the occasion of King Herod's birthday, she dances before his guests and is offered in return anything her heart desires: "And she, being before instructed of her mother, said, Give me here John Baptist's head in a charger" (Appendix A1, p. 87).[1] The story inspired several nineteenth-century adaptations, including Heinrich Heine's *Atta Troll* (1843), three dramatic poems by J.C. Heywood (whose work would be reviewed by Wilde himself), Stéphane Mallarmé's *Hérodiade* (1864-67), Gustave Flaubert's short story "Hérodias" (1877), and countless others (Appendix A3, pp. 89-91; A4, pp. 91-94; A6, pp. 95-96; A7, pp. 96-99). Collectively, these sources introduce a lurid sensuality to the story, depicting Herodias as strangely attracted to the prophet whose death she ultimately demands. An emphasis on the story's erotic subtext was thus introduced well before Wilde's play. Even his brother, William Wilde, predated Wilde's drama by composing a poem on the subject in 1878, depicting Salome as a "devouring flame" who overpowers her audience, each spectator becoming "mine, mine utterly" (Appendix A8, p. 100).

As in his brother's account, Wilde's Salome makes the grisly request for the prophet's head on her own behalf, no longer a dutiful daughter carrying out the bidding of Herodias but instead an agent of desire in her own right: "It is not my mother's voice that I heed. It is for mine own pleasure that I ask the head of Iokanaan in a silver charger" (p. 78). It is this slight alteration— the recognition of Salome's agency—that distinguishes Wilde's play from previous adaptations of it. In the original text, Salome is merely an instrument used to execute her mother's will and to satisfy Herod's prurient longing. In Wilde's adaptation, she becomes a powerful artist who is able to manipulate the actions and desires of others. These alterations, deemed by many nineteenth-century readers to be sacrilegious, to this day continue to raise important questions. Does Wilde's alteration of the original text celebrate or condemn Salome's bad behavior? Does the play

---

1 A charger is a large, flat, and often decorative platter.

constitute a revision of the sacred, or is the Biblical story merely a backdrop for Wilde's exploration of secular themes? Is *Salome* a declaration of religious defiance or a work of thoughtful exegesis?

To broach these questions, one must first consider Wilde's religious background. To associate theology with Oscar Wilde—a satirist who especially delighted in critiquing Victorian piety—might seem incongruous. As an undergraduate at Oxford University, Wilde often displayed a flippant attitude toward religious subjects. After a meeting of the Apollo Lodge one evening, he was reportedly asked to reflect upon the order's patron saint, John the Baptist (known in *Salome* by his Hebrew name, Iokanaan).[1] Wilde remarked: "we shall emulate his life but not his death—I mean we ought to keep our heads."[2] While he famously earned a double first in the Classics, Wilde failed his Divinity Examination the first time he took it, arriving late to the exam only to ridicule both the examiner and the Church of England.[3] When the proctor inquired whether he would take an exam in Divinity (Anglican doctrine) or Substituted Matter (non-Anglican doctrine), Wilde replied: "Oh, the Forty-Nine Articles." The proctor reminded him that the doctrinal position of the Anglican Church was based on the *Thirty*-Nine Articles, to which Wilde offered the glib rejoinder: "Oh, is it really?"[4]

Notwithstanding such impudent gestures, Wilde himself would repeatedly profess an interest in converting to Catholicism, from early youth to the days just preceding his death.[5] Wilde was born in 1854 to a Protestant family, though his mother, Lady Jane (known as "Speranza") Wilde, was captivated enough by Catholic ritual to have had both of her sons baptized in infancy without the consent of her husband.[6] This secret

---

1 The Apollo Lodge (founded 1818) is a Masonic lodge for members of the Oxford University community. Wilde joined on 23 February 1875.

2 Quoted in Richard Ellmann, *Oscar Wilde* (New York: Vintage Books, 1988), 40.

3 The Church of England combines elements of Catholic and Protestant tradition yet remains independent of the papacy. The Thirty-Nine Articles record the chief doctrines of Anglicanism, especially in relation to the religious controversies that characterized the English Reformation.

4 Ellmann 63. On another occasion, Wilde apparently found it "a mere dream, and very strange" that the English Church "should be so anxious to believe the Blessed Virgin conceived in sin" (*Complete Letters* 23).

5 Joseph Pearce, *The Unmasking of Oscar Wilde* (San Francisco: Ignatius Press, 2000), 392-94.

6 Ellmann 19.

baptism did not amount to a true conversion to Catholic practice, but Wilde remained fascinated by Catholicism well into his young adult life. By 1876, Lord Gower would describe Wilde as "a pleasant cheerful fellow but with his long-haired head full of nonsense regarding the Church of Rome."[1] A Catholic priest once noted that Wilde's outward flamboyance concealed a man of serious spiritual proclivities: "Behind his superficial veneer of vanity and foolish talk there is, I am convinced, something deeper and more sincere, including a genuine attraction towards Catholic belief and practice. But the time has not come. The finger of God has not yet touched him."[2]

Wilde's poetry and letters through the 1870s and 1880s are likewise replete with theological references and frank disclosures of his personal views on faith. In an 1877 letter to William Ward, then traveling in Rome, Wilde betrays uncertainty about the merits of converting, yet his words also reflect a deep reverence for the "awful fascination of the Church, its extreme beauty and sentiment":

> If I *could hope* that the Church would wake in me some earnestness and purity I would go over *as a luxury*, if for no better reasons. But I can hardly hope it would, and to go over to Rome would be to sacrifice and give up my two great gods 'Money and Ambition'.
>
> Still I get so wretched and low and troubled that in some desperate mood I will seek the shelter of a Church which simply enthralls me by its fascination.[3]

Certainly, Wilde's claim that "Money and Ambition" presented an obstacle to conversion might signal his reluctance to embrace a life of humble worship. To say that Wilde was torn between the spiritual offerings of Catholicism and the pleasures of the secular world, however, would be to oversimplify what was an incredibly complicated personal conflict. It would perhaps be better to see Wilde's early religious development as an attempt to reconcile the two, an instinct that would survive well into the 1890s, as expressed in Lord Henry Wotton's injunction to "cure the soul by means of the senses, and the senses by means of the soul."[4]

---

1 Pearce 74.

2 E.H. Mikhail, ed., *Oscar Wilde: Interviews and Recollections*, vol. 1 (New York: Barnes and Noble, 1979), 7.

3 *Complete Letters* 39.

4 Oscar Wilde, *The Picture of Dorian Gray*, *Major Works*, 47-214 (New York: Oxford UP, 2008), 63.

Although Wilde's play may seem to bring a dark sensuality to the dancing princess, who brazenly dares to kiss the cold lips of Iokanaan's severed head, it is steeped in Wilde's deep and abiding interest in cultivating a relationship between secular and spiritual desire. In other words, Wilde longed to comprehend the relationship between the sensory experience of this world—especially as reflected through art—and more abstract, intangible truths.

Wilde pursued this idea at Oxford, where he studied under two of the great aesthetic theorists of the day: John Ruskin (1819-1900) and Walter Pater (1839-94). For Wilde, Ruskin's knowledge of art was nearly inseparable from his value as a moral exemplar. In an 1888 letter to Ruskin, he remarked: "There is in you something of prophet, of priest, and of poet, and to you the gods gave eloquence such as they have given to none other, so that your message might come to us with the fire of passion, and the marvel of music, making the deaf to hear, and the blind to see."[1] Richard Ellmann has suggested that Ruskin provided a model for the "frenzied untouchable" Iokanaan, and Wilde's depiction of this messianic Ruskin certainly would seem to lend credence to this theory.[2] Ultimately, however, it was more than Ruskin's eloquence that shaped Wilde's understanding of the connection between art and religion. The material realm constituted for Ruskin a reflection of the spiritual, and much of his work endeavors to bring these two worlds into closer proximity. We see this especially in his preface to *The Seven Lamps of Architecture* (1849), where Ruskin defends himself against charges that he had blasphemed by introducing "sacred words" into his writing:

> ... my excuse must be my wish that those words were made the ground of every argument and the test of every action. We have them not often enough on our lips, nor deeply enough in our memories, nor loyally enough in our lives. The snow, the vapour, and the stormy wind fulfill His word. Are our acts and thoughts lighter and wilder than these—that we should forget it?[3]

---

1 *Complete Letters* 349.

2 Ellmann 52. Ellmann notes additionally that Wilde "knew that Ruskin had spent the summer before they met in a monastic cell at Assisi, though he refused to be converted on the grounds that he was more Catholic than the Roman Catholics" (53).

3 John Ruskin, *The Seven Lamps of Architecture* (New York: John Wiley, [1849] 1859), 5.

In such a passage, Wilde's comparison of Ruskin to a priest or prophet seems appropriate. Mingling the secular and the divine was a deliberate rhetorical move on Ruskin's part, intended to reflect the vital importance of recognizing divinity in the words and objects of everyday life.

Perhaps the most significant illustration of this approach emerged in *Stones of Venice* (1851). It is here that Ruskin famously argues that Renaissance architecture reflected the lingering influence and imminent decline of Christian values, "certain dominant evils of modern times—over-sophistication and ignorant classicalism."[1] In Ruskin's view, the Renaissance artists had abandoned the aspirational sanctity of earlier periods, mingling pagan and Christian influences in works of art that were consequently irregular, indeterminate, and spiritually vapid. Walter Pater, also teaching at Oxford at the time, would revise this idea in his seminal work, *The Renaissance* (1873). Although agreeing that the Renaissance reflected an attempt to reconcile the pagan and Christian traditions in art, Pater admired the result as the gratifying union of seemingly opposed impulses—it was, he averred, the birth of decadence. Speaking of Leonardo da Vinci's sketches of women, a series he suggestively describes as "Daughters of Herodias," Pater observes:

> They are the clairvoyants through whom, as through delicate instruments, one becomes aware of the subtler forces of nature, and the modes of their action, all that is magnetic in it, all those finer conditions wherein material things rise to that subtlety of operation which constitutes them spiritual, where only the finer nerve and the keener touch can follow. It is as if in certain significant examples we actually saw those forces at their work on human flesh.[2]

If Ruskin maintained that one may discern traces of divinity in this world, Pater proposed that material reality is coextensive with divinity—that the senses are themselves evidence of divine power.[3] Despite their differences, then, Wilde's tutors shared a

---

1 John Ruskin, *Stones of Venice*, *The Genius of John Ruskin: Selections from His Writings*, ed. John D. Rosenberg (Charlottesville: U of Virginia P, 1964), 149.

2 Walter Pater, *The Renaissance*, ed. Donald L. Hill (Berkeley: U of California P, 1980), 91.

3 Discussions of the comparison can be found in Ellmann (47-52) and in Kenneth Daley's detailed study, *The Rescue of Romanticism: Walter Pater and John Ruskin* (Columbus: Ohio State UP, 2001).

commitment to clarifying the relationship between material reality and hidden truths—a commitment that Wilde himself would pursue and adapt in *Salome*.[1]

The often overlooked dialogue among the Jews in *Salome* is a notable case in point. Having been told that Iokanaan is "a man who has seen God," Herod's guests speculate on the possibility of any man's seeking an audience with the divine. While one proclaims that "In these days God doth not show himself," another asserts: "God is at no time hidden. He showeth Himself at all times and in all places. God is in what is evil even as He is in what is good" (p. 67). A diligent scholar of theosophy and the occult, Wilde invokes in this passage a distinctly Gnostic worldview.[2] According to the early Gnostics, the material world consisted of both good and evil elements, which could only be disentangled through the pursuit of higher spiritual knowledge. As John Harris notes, "At the heart of *gnosis* there is mystery, the mystery of the divine secretive purpose for the world," the pursuit of which "testifies to the human quest for enlightenment on the dilemmas of life in a materialistic world and the means of release from it."[3] With its focus on the pursuit of knowledge, Gnosticism refuses a monolithic view of the world and, indeed, invites precisely the kind of debate and deliberation we witness among the guests at Herod's court. Hence, the fifth Jew calls attention to the obscurity of all religious knowledge, observing: "No man can tell how God worketh. His ways are very dark. It may be that the things which we call evil are good, and that the things which we call good are evil. There is no knowledge of anything" (p. 68). Wilde pointedly resists resolution and instead presents the audience with a series of possibilities: the divine is hidden, the divine is present in all things, or we can never acquire true knowledge of the divine. In *Salome*, as in so many of Wilde's plays, knowledge is not meant to be acquired—true to the Gnostic tradition, it is the pursuit of mystery, rather than revelation, that bears real spiritual fruit.

---

1 Another important Victorian touchstone for the idea that the physical world would symbolically reflect the metaphysical is Thomas Carlyle, who proposed in *Sartor Resartus* (1833-34) a "Philosophy of Clothes" that presented all visible phenomena—including language itself—as an emanation of the divine.

2 See Jarlath Killeen, *The Fairy Tales of Oscar Wilde* (London: Ashgate, 2013).

3 John Glyndwr Harris, *Gnosticism: Beliefs and Practices* (Sussex: Sussex Academic Press, 1999), 1.

To some extent, this helps to explain the text's constant attention to what is "hidden": the gods who "have hidden themselves in the mountains," the centaurs who "have hidden themselves in the rivers," or the face of Salome "hidden [...] behind her fan" (pp. 79, 53, 51). Although Wilde invites us to imagine these objects, they remain concealed from view, deliberately provoking yet refusing to satisfy our curiosity.[1] The advantage of such a strategy is that it invites the reader to engage in an unremitting process of reflection, discovery, and self-making. After all, as Wilde himself observes in "The Critic as Artist," the contemplative life is "the life that has for its aim not *doing* but *being*, and not *being* merely, but *becoming*."[2] By this logic, the reader who fails to ask questions falls into a kind of intellectual stasis; the reader who is repeatedly confronted by mystery becomes, by the same token, a dynamic and reflective agent of action.

Wilde's poetry reflects this emphasis on the value of pursuing mystery even more pointedly. To offer only one example, we might turn to "Rome Unvisited" (1875). At the time of the poem's composition, Wilde was traveling with J.M. Mahaffy, the tutor at Trinity College who first introduced him to the Greeks. George Macmillan mentioned in a letter to his father that Wilde was journeying to Rome "to see all the glories of the religion which seems to him the highest and the most sentimental."[3] Wilde soon after wrote to Macmillan, explaining that he "never went to Rome at all," Mahaffy having diverted him to Greece. This alteration in his itinerary seems to have left a mark on Wilde, whose poem expresses a lingering desire

> [...] to see before I die
> The only God-anointed King,
> And hear the silver trumpets ring
> A triumph as He passes by!

---

1   John Stokes has proposed that "the reason why Wilde loved mystery so much is, paradoxically, that he was at heart a rationalist, willing to accept that scientific discovery could offer an increasingly adequate account of the visible world" (3). Certainly, Stokes is right to suggest that Wilde did not recommend a passive or detached relationship to mystery—the unseen is meant to be approached, pursued, and engaged. Yet the ultimate aim of such a pursuit, for Wilde, is not necessarily resolution. Indeed, it is the power of mystery to stimulate thought itself that Wilde prizes above all else. See John Stokes, *Oscar Wilde: Myths, Miracles, Imitations* (Cambridge: Cambridge UP, 1996).

2   Oscar Wilde, "The Critic as Artist. Part II," *Major Works* 267-98. 277.

3   Wilde, *Complete Letters* 44.

Or at the brazen-pillared shrine
Holds high the mystic sacrifice
And shows his God to human eyes
Beneath the veil of bread and wine.[1]

Wilde's fascination with religion seems to have been informed by a passion for spectacle (the celebrity of the Pope, the blaring of "silver trumpets"), a genuine reverence for divinity, and a decided attraction to spiritual mystery. His mention of the "veil of bread and wine" is especially suggestive. In *Salome*, Wilde would become the first to describe Salome's performance before Herod as the "dance of the seven veils." The imagery of the veil is often thought to reflect what is concealed from human view, yet in "Rome Unvisited," Wilde suggests that the veil might also serve as a form of communication between the divine and the secular, thus representing both mystery and revelation in a single breath.

Certainly, such an understanding of Salome's veils is reinforced by the play's repeated allusions to the Veil of the Sanctuary, which at the Temple of Jerusalem concealed the inner sanctum housing the Ark of the Covenant. The Gospels report that the veil was torn when Christ was crucified, a visible signal of the ensuing rift between the secular and the divine. In Wilde's play, Herodias accuses Herod of stealing the Veil of the Sanctuary (p. 73), and the charge is later verified by Herod's offering Salome the Veil in exchange for her dance. If the Veil represents the possibility of communication between the secular and the divine, then Herod's displacement of it suggests the refusal of such communication—the Veil's chief value, for Herod, is its rarity, and possession of it reflects his own power. Indeed, one of Herod's signature qualities is his covetous nature. Herod's assurance that he can give Salome anything she wishes from his collection of treasures reinforces his insistence that he can lay claim to anything he likes, including her body. Far from embracing mystery, then, Herod acquires, dominates, and confines the objects of his desire, from his "beautiful white peacocks" to Iokanaan himself, whom he imprisons in the cistern—yet another object in his exotic collection—despite suspecting that he may be a true prophet (p. 80). Herod's possession of the Veil, like his possession of Iokanaan, suggests a failure to adequately broach the relationship between material and spiritual value.

1 Oscar Wilde, "Rome Unvisited," *The Complete Poetry* (Oxford: Oxford UP, 2009), 5-6.

It is worth noting that only two years after writing "Rome Unvisited," Wilde did finally make it to Rome and even met Pope Pius IX. Wilde was rendered uncharacteristically speechless by the encounter, though he was reportedly even more awestruck at the grave of John Keats, which he deemed "the holiest place in Rome."[1] These vacillations between the divine and the secular signal the difficulty of assigning to Wilde either a wholehearted commitment to religious thought or rejection of it. Indeed, in a letter to Lord Houghton describing his visit to Keats's grave, Wilde observes: "Someway standing by his grave I felt that he *too* was a Martyr, and worthy to lie in the City of Martyrs. I thought of him as a Priest of Beauty slain before his time [...]."[2] For Wilde, then, poetry and religion served similar functions: both illuminated while also preserving the mysterious connection between this world and the unseen, often inaccessible, truth that underlies it. Wilde valued mystery because it prompts the kind of intellectual movement and reflection that fosters self-development. It is this preoccupation that explains that apparent contradiction in Wilde's personality: his simultaneous attraction to Catholicism and to the more profane luxuries of this world. It is, moreover, this conflation of spiritual longing and poetic indulgence that defines Wilde's provocative aesthetic in *Salomé*.

Symbolism and the Senses

As Wilde sought to bridge the distance between material and metaphysical reality, he found himself mediating other types of boundaries as well. Wilde wrote *Salome* while living in Paris, ensconced in the world of the French symbolists, several of whom played an active role in the play's development. Originally, the term "symbolism" was coined by Jean Moréas in his 1886 manifesto, which describes its proponents as "enemies of teaching, declamation, false sensibility, and objective description" who insisted upon the power of the imagination and of dreams to access concealed truth.[3] In effect, they sought to address stylistically precisely those questions that had characterized Wilde's early reflections on religion. Building deliberately on the work of the German pessimists—especially Arthur Schopenhauer,

---

1 Wilde, *Complete Letters* 247.
2 Wilde, *Complete Letters* 49.
3 Jean Moréas, "The Symbolist Manifesto," *European Literature from Romanticism to Postmodernism: A Reader in Aesthetic Practice*, ed. Martin Travers, 147-49 (London: Bloomsbury Publishing, 2006), 148.

Friedrich Hegel, and Eduard von Hartmann—the symbolists were attracted by art's ability to provide access to concealed truth. According to the symbolists, "depictions of nature, human actions, indeed all concrete phenomena should not show themselves as such: they are outward forms, whose purpose is to represent their hidden affinities with primordial Ideas."[1] As Moréas observes, the symbolist approach depends upon

> an archetypal and complex style: unpolluted words, clear phrasing which will act as a buttress, and alternate with others of undulating faintness, with signifying pleonasms, mysterious ellipses, and the anacoluthon left in suspense, every trope daring and multiform; and finally, good French— restored and modernized ...[2]

The symbolists thus advocated displacing conventional rhetoric through a deliberate appeal to simplicity, redundancy ("signifying pleonasms"), fluidity of meaning ("mysterious ellipses"), and deviations from normal syntax ("anacoluthon"). In combination, these devices helped to transport the reader from a concrete and seemingly familiar landscape to one where new questions, insights, and modes of thinking become possible.

Wilde turned to such strategies frequently in *Salome*. The opening lines of the play offer a clear illustration of symbolist principles:

FIRST SOLDIER. The Tetrarch has a sombre aspect.

SECOND SOLDIER. Yes; he has a sombre aspect.

FIRST SOLDIER. He is looking at something.

SECOND SOLDIER. He is looking at someone.

FIRST SOLDIER. At whom is he looking?

SECOND SOLDIER. I cannot tell.

THE YOUNG SYRIAN. How pale the Princess is! Never have I seen her so pale. She is like the shadow of a white rose in a mirror of silver. (p. 48)

The almost rhythmic style of this passage has often been attributed to the influence of Maurice Maeterlinck, a figure instru-

---

1 Moréas 148.
2 Moréas 149.

mental in adapting symbolist techniques to the stage (Appendix A10, pp. 105-06). Here, the simplicity of Wilde's syntax is reinforced by repeated claims that Herod "has a sombre aspect" and "is looking" at someone or something. Yet this clear and unadulterated mode of expression is ultimately disrupted by the Young Syrian's somewhat startling revelation that Salome is "like the shadow of a white rose in a mirror of silver," a layering of images that both attracts and challenges the audience's visual imagination. How, we might ask, is the shadow of a white rose different from the shadow of a red rose? What does a shadow look like in a mirror? How do we reconcile the image of a dark shadow with a bright reflection? Perhaps most importantly, what does it signify that Salome herself is described as something both visible and lacking substance?

The play's preoccupation with demonstrating a connection between the seen and the unseen is reinforced by the play's structural elements.[1] Especially suggestive is Wilde's use of ellipses at moments when the characters struggle to articulate their thoughts or desires. The Young Syrian, for instance, is so rapt by Salome's beauty that he struggles to affix a single meaning to it: "She is like a dove that has strayed.... She is like a narcissus trembling in the wind.... She is like a silver flower ..." (p. 52). As the Young Syrian's passion for Salome eludes description, the ellipses stand in as visible emblems of concealed or deferred knowledge. Salome's addresses to Iokanaan likewise include multiple ellipses as she searches for the best way to articulate her longing for him, and a similar pattern emerges in Herod's attempts to persuade Salome to accept material wealth (rather than the decapitated head of Iokanaan) as payment for her dance (pp. 79-82). Rhetorically, then, the use of ellipses reflects the pursuit of an elusive object one desperately pursues but can never possess. At the very moment Wilde's characters struggle to articulate or affix meaning, they are reminded of the impossibility of doing so, reinforcing the limitations of "clothing the Idea in sensuous form."[2] An evolving understanding of the possibilities and limits of symbolic thinking thus becomes a central focus for the play's characters. Although the moon is likened to "a dead woman," a "little princess who wears a yellow veil," a "little piece of money," "a mad woman," a "virgin," and more, Herodias suggests that "the

---

1 For a discussion of Wilde's use of musical language in *Salome*, see David Wayne Thomas, "The 'Strange Music' of *Salome*: Oscar Wilde's Rhetoric of Verbal Musicality," *Mosaic* 33.1 (March 2000): 15-38.

2 Moréas 148.

moon is like the moon, that is all" (p. 64). Herod too ultimately sees the potential dangers of a too fixed interpretation of the symbols he sees around him. As he awaits Salome's dance, he observes: "How red those petals are! They are like stains of blood on the cloth. That does not matter. It is not wise to find symbols in everything that one sees. It makes life too full of terrors. It were better to say that stains of blood are as lovely as rose-petals. It were better far to say that.... But we will not speak of this" (p. 76).

Wilde's skepticism here reflects, at bottom, a concern with the limitations symbols place on thought itself. It is dangerous to assign a single meaning to any object, for to do so is to arrest the process of reflection that makes growth and transformation possible. In Wilde's view, it is far more productive to mediate constantly between the material world and the many possible truths it might purvey. This concept is borne out by Wilde's fascination with visual renderings of Salome in the time leading up to the play's composition, which is documented in detail by Guatemalan writer Gomez Carillo (1873-1927). According to Carillo, Wilde spoke incessantly of depictions of Salome by Titian, Massimo Stanzioni, Alessandro Veronese, Peter Paul Rubens, Albrecht Dürer, Domenico Ghirlandaio, Callisto Piazza, Theodoor Van Thulden, Henri Regnault, Paul de Saint Victor, Jean Leclerc, Leonardo da Vinci, and Gustave Moreau. As Carillo puts it, "there were ten, no, a hundred Salomes that he imagined, that he began, that he abandoned. Each painting he saw in a museum suggested a new idea; each book he found in which the object of his interest was mentioned filled him with self-doubts."[1] Indeed, few visual renderings of Salome seemed to be to his liking. While Wilde admired Titian's "Salome with the head of John the Baptist" (c. 1515), he apparently found Peter Paul Rubens's buxom princess to be too much of this world, "a sluttish woman who was about to have an attack of apoplexy."[2] By contrast, Wilde regarded Leonardo da Vinci's Salome—a slight woman of wan complexion who averts her gaze from the head of John the Baptist—as "too reserved and other-worldly."[3] If Rubens depicts a Salome who was too fleshly and material for Wilde's taste, da Vinci's painting suggests a similarly troubling repudiation of the senses. In Wilde's view, it would seem, existing

---

1 Mikhail 194.
2 Mikhail 195.
3 Ibid. Wilde was most likely thinking of Giampietrino's painting of Salome after da Vinci's "Leda and the Swan," long presumed lost.

depictions of Salome's body tended to be either too voluptuous or too angelic.

Significantly, Wilde rejected both interpretations of the Salome myth, preferring instead the paintings of Gustave Moreau (Appendix B1, p. 108), who seems to have shared Wilde's obsession, having completed three different paintings and countless early studies of the mysterious princess. Joris-Karl Huysmans provides a detailed description of Moreau's work in *À Rebours* (1884), a work that also informed *The Picture of Dorian Gray*.[1] For Des Esseintes, the hero of *À Rebours*, the Gospels failed to capture "the refined grandeur of this murderess." Instead, they rendered her "vague and hidden, mysterious and swooning in the far-off mist of the centuries, not to be grasped by vulgar and materialistic minds [...] rebellious to painters of the flesh." As represented by Moreau, Salome became a different creature altogether:

> She was no longer the mere performer who wrests a cry of desire and of passion from an old man by a perverted twisting of her loins; who destroys the energy and breaks the will of a king by trembling breasts and quivering belly. She became, in a sense, the symbolic deity of indestructible lust, the goddess of immortal Hysteria, of accursed Beauty, distinguished from all others by the catalepsy which stiffens her flesh and hardens her muscles; the monstrous Beast, indifferent, irresponsible, insensible, baneful, like the Helen of antiquity, fatal to all who approach her, all who behold her, all whom she touches. (Appendix A9, p. 102)

Rejecting both the muted Salome of Scripture and the corporeal spectacle set forth by "painters of the flesh" like Rubens, Des Esseintes finds in Moreau's painting a Salome who communicates desire as both bodily and transcendent.

Wilde shared Moreau's ecstatic vision of Salome. According to Carillo, he reflected at length on the visual spectacle of Salome's body, imagining it to be both sensual and mystical—and not merely the object but also the agent of desire:

---

1   Wilde noted to E.W. Pratt in 1892 that Dorian Gray's yellow book "is partly suggested by Huysmans' *À Rebours*, which you will get at any French bookseller's. It is a fantastic variation on Huysmans' over-realistic study of the artistic temperament in our inartistic age" (*Complete Letters* 524).

Yes, he continued, utterly naked. But with jewels, many jewels, interlacing strands of jewels; all the gems flashing, tinkling a jingling at her ankles, her wrists, her arms, about her neck, around her waist; their reflections making the utter shamelessness of that warm flesh even more shocking. For I cannot conceive of a Salome who is unconscious of what she does, a Salome who is but a silent and passive instrument.... Never ...! [...] Her beauty has nothing of this world about it.... Thin veils woven by the angels wrap round her slender figure. The golden waves of her hair conceal the delights of her neck. Her eyes shine and sparkle, and are the very stars of hope or faith.[1]

For Wilde, as for Moreau, Salome is profoundly sensual and yet seems to enter the world from another and less familiar world. Numinous and bright, while also tangible and earthly, the Salome of Moreau's "The Apparition" broaches the divide between the senses and the otherworldly. Wilde's investment in visual sources should not therefore lead us to believe that his understanding of desire is purely corporeal. On the contrary, Salome's dance of the seven veils, like all art in Wilde's view, provokes contemplation of what remains unseen and, in so doing, denotes the possibility of personal transformation.

Wilde sought to reinforce this effect by appealing to another symbolist concept, synesthesia—a holistic sensory experience that calls simultaneously upon sight, touch, smell, sound, and taste to create a more dynamic aesthetic experience. Charles Ricketts, an artist and writer in his own right, was asked to design the set for the original performance of *Salome* in consultation with Wilde. Although the performance never took place, Ricketts's plans for the set reflect a clear interest in appealing to color:

I proposed a black floor, upon which Salome's feet could move like white doves; this was said to capture the author. The sky was to be a rich turquoise green, cut by the perpendicular fall of gilded strips of Japanese matting forming an aerial tent above the terraces. Did Wilde suggest the division of the actors into separate masses of colour? To-day I cannot decide. The Jews were to be in yellow, John in white, and Herod and Herodias in blood-red. Over Salome the discussions were endless; Should she be clothed in black—like the

1 Mikhail 193.

night, in silver like the moon or—the suggestion was Wilde's—green like a curious poisonous lizard. (Appendix E1, p. 131)

Although this was a plan Wilde himself seems to have endorsed, he wished to take the sensory experience of the drama even further. According to Graham Robertson, Wilde wanted to complement the visual spectacle of the play with a pageant of olfactory sensations: "... in place of an orchestra, braziers of perfume. Think—the scented clouds rising and partly veiling the stage from time to time—a new perfume for each emotion" (Appendix E2, p. 132). Coupled with the musicality of *Salome*—the rhythmic pauses, ellipses, and structural idiosyncrasies of Wilde's syntax—the play continually calls upon the audience to reflect on how desire is embodied and, in keeping with symbolist principles, how the senses can lead us to an unseen and potentially transformative reality.

Such a reading gains credence when set alongside Wilde's symbolist poem "La Fuite de la Lune":

To outer senses there is peace,
A dreamy peace on either hand
Deep silence in the shadowy land,
Deep silence where the shadows cease.

Save for a cry that echoes shrill
From some lone bird disconsolate;
A corncrake calling to its mate;
The answer from the misty hill.

And suddenly the moon withdraws
Her sickle from the lightening skies,
And to her sombre cavern flies,
Wrapped in a veil of yellow gauze.[1]

Imitating the French symbolists, Wilde here represents a nocturnal scene that is silent, dark, and concealed from the "outer senses." This scene is interrupted by the cry of a bird "calling to its mate" through the darkness, seeking to establish contact with a companion who remains unseen and inaccessible. As if to signal the significance of this effort at transcending the visible world,

---

1   Oscar Wilde, "La Fuite de la Lune," *Complete Poetry* 131.

the moon recoils, "wrapped in a veil of yellow gauze," a gesture that recognizes those "echoes shrill" that disrupt the seemingly placid, shadowy nightscape. Paradoxically, the moon constitutes the first and only concrete visual image of the poem, and yet remains curiously concealed from view. The moon and the veil, both images that feature prominently in *Salome*, reflect how an attempt at connection might produce illumination and bewilderment at the same time. The poem, much like *Salome* itself, seems to collapse multiple senses into an impression of deliberate, provocative, and productive obfuscation.

If Wilde thematizes the inaccessibility and unknowability of desire, then, this is not a state of affairs he laments. Wilde presents the aesthetic experience not merely as an escape from an otherwise futile search for truth—that unending pursuit of knowledge is itself the thing to be sought after. In the words of Keats: "beauty is truth, truth beauty."[1] There is perhaps no better example of this principle than Salome's body itself. Described variously as like "the shadow of a white rose in a mirror of silver," "a dove that has strayed," "a narcissus trembling in the wind," and "a silver flower" (pp. 48, 52), Salome's body is continually subject to metaphorical description. The use of simile is suggestive, for simile only ever claims to articulate truth by analogy—a simile tells us what something is *like* but does not expressly tell us what it *is*. As the similes used to describe Salome multiply—as she comes to resemble objects that are essentially unlike one another—her body eludes description and becomes, as Helen Davies would have it, a kind of "free-floating signifier."[2] Salome's body serves as a canvas upon which the spectator (or reader) projects a meaning that can never be apprehended as fully and literally true. While the play overflows with comparisons that seem full of symbolic meaning, nothing objectively "true" is ever established through them. The figure of Salome performing the dance of the seven veils thus becomes a reflection upon what the drama can accomplish—its ability to convey through mobility, sensation, and obscurity the very difficult work of interpreting the world in which we live.

Curiously, though, Salome is also the most brash transgressor against Wilde's aesthetic. Even as Salome's body reflects the buoyancy of unfulfilled longing—for love, knowledge, or power—

---

1 John Keats, "Ode on a Grecian Urn," *The Complete Poems* (New York: Penguin, 1977), 346.

2 Helen Davies, "The Trouble with Gender in *Salomé*," Michael Bennett, *Refiguring Oscar Wilde's Salome*, 55-70 (New York: Rodopi, 2011), 276.

Salome herself fails to grasp Wilde's Keatsian aesthetic. Requesting the head of Iokanaan on a silver charger, she means to look upon the face that refused her—to kiss the lips that once pronounced such mysterious prophecies. Yet the scene is hardly a victory for Salome. The similes she once used to describe her desire suddenly become as rigid and expressionless as the severed head upon which she gazes. When Salome first addresses the strange, disembodied voice of Iokanaan, her language is searching and figurative: "Thy body is hideous. It is *like* the body of a leper. It is *like* a plastered wall, where vipers have crawled; *like* a plastered wall where the scorpions have made their nest. It is *like* a whited sepulcher, full of loathsome things" (p. 60; emphasis added). When she later addresses Iokanaan's severed head, her language becomes more fixed: "Thy body *was* a column of ivory set upon feet of silver. It *was* a garden full of doves and lilies of silver. It *was* a tower of silver decked with shields of ivory" (p. 84; emphasis added). The shift to the past tense and to metaphor affix and arrest her desire, which is no longer aspirational and mobile but instead static and frail. If Salome is "punished" at the end of the play, then, it is by no means clear that she is punished solely for her transgression against God or against the tetrarch. Indeed, her gravest infraction seems to be her departure from the aesthetic mode Wilde sets out to reveal and celebrate in the play. Salome's attempt to affix meaning and to arrest the lips that once uttered mysterious prophecies suggests that she is not so different from Herod after all—she too fails to fully grasp that to possess beauty is to destroy it.

Translation and Suppression

Of course, one of Moréas's chief claims in "The Symbolist Manifesto" was that the works of this aesthetic "renaissance" be articulated in "good French—restored and modernized."[1] Wilde's decision to compose *Salome* in French might well be regarded as an homage to the writers whose company had ushered the play into existence. Yet his affinity for French also reflects a philosophical and aesthetic choice. In an interview for the *Pall Mall Budget*, Wilde noted: "A great deal of the curious effect that Maeterlinck produces comes from the fact that he, a Flamand by race, writes in an alien language. The same thing is true of [Dante Gabriel] Rossetti who, though he wrote in English, was essen-

1 Moréas 148, 149.

tially Latin in temperament" (Appendix E6, p. 137). In a letter to Edmond de Goncourt, Wilde went on to observe: "One can adore a language without speaking it well, as one can love a woman without understanding her. French by sympathy, I am Irish by race, and the English have condemned me to speak the language of Shakespeare."[1]

Wilde's appreciation of French culture, as well as his popularity in France, have been well-documented.[2] To some extent, the sympathy between French symbolism and British aestheticism permitted Wilde to adopt France as a cultural homeland. Indeed, when *Salome* was banned from the stage, he threatened to formally renounce England in order to become a French citizen (Appendix E6, p. 137). Ultimately, though, Wilde's use of the French language seems to have dovetailed with his interest in cultivating a distinct aesthetic experience—one that would defamiliarize language in order to afford it a quality both material and transcendent. During the composition of *Salome*, he noted to Florence Balcome Stoker that it was a "strange venture in a tongue that is not my own," but that he loved "as one loves an instrument of music on which one has not played before."[3] Wilde took his experiment in the French language quite seriously; upon presenting a draft of the play to Stuart Merrill, Adolphe Retté, and Pierre Louÿs, Wilde requested that they "eliminate any glaring anglicisms."[4] According to Retté, the circle was initially receptive to his project: "One day Merrill said to me: 'Wilde would like you and me to take pen in hand and read the manuscript of his play Salomé to take out those anglicisms which are too explicit. I don't share his view, for it's precisely the exotic nature of Wilde's French which seems to me to be one of the attractions of the play. However, Wilde insists on it.'"[5] In the end, Retté seems to have been encouraging, while Merrill was aggravated by Wilde's constant repetition of certain words—precisely those "pleonasms" that Moréas had celebrated—and by "a

---

1 Oscar Wilde, *Selected Letters*, ed. Rupert Hart-Davis (New York: Oxford UP, 1979), 100.

2 See Richard Hibbett, "The Artist as Aesthete: The French Creation of Oscar Wilde," in Stefano Evangelista, *The Reception of Oscar Wilde in Europe* (New York: Continuum, 2010), 65-79; Emily Eells, "Naturalizing Oscar Wilde as an *homme de lettres*: The French Reception of *Dorian Gray* and *Salomé* (1895-1922), in Evangelista 80-95.

3 Wilde, *Complete Letters* 552.

4 Donohue, "Translator's Preface" xi.

5 Mikhail 190.

certain perceived awkwardness" in his use of French.[1] Regardless of Merrill's concerns, the ultimate effect—the defamiliarization of common words and concepts—seems to have been a success, at least among French-speaking audiences. In the words of Wilde's longtime friend and literary executor, Robert Ross: "Salomé has made the author's name a household word wherever the English language is not spoken."[2]

Indeed, much of the "perceived awkwardness" and repetition appears to have been a deliberate strategy on Wilde's part, as his dispute with Lord Alfred Douglas regarding the first English translation of the play suggests. Wilde's lover at the time of the play's composition, Douglas agreed to translate *Salome*, though Wilde was ultimately disappointed by the result, noting that it was full of "school boy faults" and "as unworthy of you, as an ordinary Oxonian, as it was of the work it sought to render" (Appendix D3, p. 124). Ultimately, Wilde himself took the translation in hand, amending Douglas's French in several key instances. More than likely, however, Wilde was not merely disappointed by Douglas's technical limitations as a translator. The license Douglas took with the English translation undermined Wilde's interest in thematizing the relationship between mystery, art, and desire. As Appendix D6 indicates, the most notable alterations introduced by Douglas into the English translation of the play relate specifically to those details that constitute deliberate cultural and stylistic choices on Wilde's part. For instance, in the original text, Herod recalls Iokanaan's prophecy: "Il a prédit que la lune deviendrait rouge comme du sang." Whereas Douglas suggests that Iokanaan foretold that the "moon would become as blood," later translations (for instance, those of Ross and Ellmann) translate the passage more accurately: "He prophesied that the moon would become *red* as blood" (emphasis added). In addition to maintaining the integrity of the original text, the appeal to color helps to reinforce the visual spectacle that Wilde, following the French symbolists, celebrates throughout the play. Elsewhere, Douglas's translation denies the text's other noteworthy cultural birthright—British aestheticism. Translating the French "lis" (literally, "lily") as "rose," Douglas curiously omits from the text the flower that was famously associated with the British aesthetes.

---

1   Donohue, "Translator's Preface" xi.
2   Robert Ross, "A Note on *Salomé*," *Salome*, trans. Lord Alfred Douglas (Los Angeles: Indo-European Publishing 2010), 1-7. 1.

Douglas's translation was republished in 1906, 1907, and 1912, each time after additional changes presumably introduced by Robert Ross (selections from Ross's translation, along with excerpts from Richard Ellmann's 1982 translation of the play, also appear in Appendix D). Over the years, this was followed by an edition issued by the Folio Society in 1957 and translated by Wilde's youngest son, Vyvyan Holland. It is worth noting that the play has subsequently been translated into dozens of languages. In 1902, Hedwig Lachmann translated *Salome* into German for Max Reinhardt's production of the play at Berlin's Kleines Theater. Richard Strauss attended this production, which inspired him to write his famous operatic rendition of the story, using Lachmann's translation as the libretto. Joseph Donohue, who attempted to translate the play into twenty-first-century American-English, notes the impossibility of imitating "the 'foreign' component of Wilde's foreign-language French."[1] Appropriately, Wilde's play seems to defy translation or reproduction. The play's thematization of the tension between form and content—body and soul, secular and divine truth—is echoed in the frustrated efforts of translators to reveal the "true" meaning of Wilde's language. In other words, these repeated attempts to arrive at a "correct" translation of the play not only testify to the play's enduring influence; they also reflect the degree to which Wilde's language, like his central character, resists fixed assignations of meaning.

These attempts at translating Wilde's language are only to be rivaled by Aubrey Beardsley's controversial visual interpretation of *Salome*. Beardsley's illustration of Salome gazing at the severed head of Iokanann, later titled "The Climax," was originally published in *The Salon*. Wilde was impressed by the image and sent a copy of the play to Beardsley with the following inscription: "For the only artist who, besides myself, knows what the dance of the seven veils is, and can see that invisible dance" (*Letters* 348, n. 3). Wilde subsequently requested that Beardsley produce a series of illustrations to accompany the first English edition of the play. When Beardsley completed his commission, Wilde was disappointed. But why? After all, in several respects, Beardsley's illustrations would seem to reinforce the aesthetic of Wilde's language. In "The Climax," for instance, Beardsley creates a landscape reminiscent of the defamiliarized, dreamlike mode of the symbolists (Appendix B5, p. 112). The conflation of art and

---

1 Donohue, "Translator's Preface" xxii.

beauty on the one hand (reflected by the lily springing up into the foreground) is sharply contrasted to the sinister image of Salome kissing the dead lips of Iokanaan. The image is provocative, stylized, mystifying, and reflects Wilde's own investment in art as a way of accessing inarticulable and sometimes disturbing realities. A 1907 review for *The Conservator* notes that in both the text and image, we can "see exquisite unsurpassed organization, verbal prestidigitation. Pictures magnificently perverted. The effect while phantomnal is not false. It is like getting a dream perspective on the truth."[1]

Yet several of Beardsley's other illustrations chafe against Wilde's belief in the higher function of art. In some cases, Beardsley's drawings focus explicitly on the body as flesh, leading Wilde to describe them as akin to the "naughty scribbles a precocious boy makes in the margins of his copybook."[2] Beardsley's original design for the title page, for instance, features a hermaphroditic daemon, which was ultimately replaced by a more sanitized female figure (Appendix B2, p. 109, and B3, p. 110). While he would continue to admire Beardsley's originality, Wilde felt that these illustrations reeked of sin and bodily excess: "When I have before me one of your drawings, I want to drink absinthe, which changes colour like jade in sunlight and makes the senses thrall, and then I can live myself back in ancient Rome, in the Rome of the later Caesars."[3] Although Wilde certainly had a reputation for indulgence, his remark suggests that Beardsley's illustrations take this to the extreme, reflecting the kind of cultural decline characteristic of Rome's final days.

Wilde was further repulsed by what he perceived as a petty, personal attack. In "The Woman in the Moon," the face of the moon bears features strikingly reminiscent of Wilde (and even wears what appears to be a carnation, the flower famously donned by Wilde and his disciples), thus drawing attention away from the text and toward the author himself (Appendix B4, p. 111). Committed to the aesthetic experience as a subjective one in which the individual would be free to enrich and develop a unique identity, Wilde was resolutely skeptical of works bearing traces of authorial intention—in other words, he rejected art that sought to convey a particular line of thought, feeling that such works failed to realize the real object of aesthetic experience. In

---

1   "Salome," *The Conservator* (September 1907), 109.
2   Barbara Belford, *Oscar Wilde: A Certain Genius* (New York: Random House, 2000), 205.
3   Belford 204.

The Picture of Dorian Gray, the artist Basil Hallward refuses to exhibit his portrait of Dorian precisely because he fears that he has "put too much of myself into it."[1] "To reveal art," Wilde insists, "and conceal the artist is art's aim."[2] To place Wilde directly into the landscape of his own work was therefore not merely unflattering—many of the images featuring Wilde are languid, corpulent, and unbecoming—but actually challenged Wilde's attempt to create a work of art that moves beyond the concerns of this world and encourages independent thought. It is in this spirit that Robert Ross described Beardsley's drawings as "a mordant, though decorative, satire on the play."[3]

The performance history of *Salome*, by the same token, reflects just how pervasive Wilde's reputation as a libertine was at the time. Wilde was determined to stage *Salome* with the incomparable Sarah Bernhardt in the starring role (Appendix E3, pp. 132-33). Only two weeks into rehearsals, however, the Examiner of Plays banned *Salome*, claiming that it violated a long-standing prohibition against staging biblical subjects. Under the authority of the Lord Chamberlain and the Theatres Act of 1843, the Examiner of Plays was empowered to ban performances when "it is fitting for the preservation of good manners, decorum or of the public peace so to do," a charge that naturally left much room for interpretation.[4] Wilde suspected that the decision was an assault on himself. The Examiner of Plays, Edward F. Smyth Pigott, had approved Charles Brookfield's *The Poet and the Puppets*, a farce making direct attacks on Wilde and spoofing *Lady Windermere's Fan*, which was then being produced at the St. James's Theatre. How could it be that libelous insults were deemed acceptable subjects for the stage, Wilde protested, whereas the noble stories of Scripture were regarded as inappropriate? In an interview for *Pall Mall Budget*, Wilde lamented: "The artistic treatment of moral and elevating subjects is discouraged, while a free course is given to the representation of disgusting and revolting subjects" (Appendix E6, p. 136). Wilde's dispute with the Lord Chamberlain cut to the very heart of his frustration with English culture. *Salome* challenged audiences to move beyond the world as it exists—with its moral strictures, institu-

---

1 Oscar Wilde, *The Picture of Dorian Gray* 133.
2 Ibid., 48.
3 Ross 5.
4 Great Britain, Proprietor of the Law Journal Reports, *The Public General Acts*, "An Act for Regulating Theatres," Cap. 68.14 (London: 1843), 129.

tions, and practical impediments—to embrace a world of new possibilities. That Pigott refused the possibility of such a world was itself a violation of Wilde's aesthetic principles. If Pigott saw in the play "a miracle of impudence, ... half-biblical, half-pornographic," Wilde averred, this reflected less the corruption of *Salome* than Pigott's own self-corruption (Appendix E4, p. 134). As Lord Henry Wotton observes in *The Picture of Dorian Gray*, "The books that the world calls immoral are books that *show the world its own shame.*"[1]

This argument was one that Wilde would recycle in the courtroom only a few years later. By the 1890s, Wilde (now married and the father of two sons) was romantically involved with Lord Alfred Douglas, a young aristocrat and aspiring poet. Douglas's father, the Marquess of Queensberry, was staunchly opposed to the relationship. In 1894, Queensberry visited Wilde's home and openly accused him of sodomy, threatening to "thrash" him if Douglas and Wilde were seen together again in public.[2] The following year, at the opening of *The Importance of Being Earnest*, he left a "large bouquet made of vegetables" for Wilde, intended as a slight to the now enormously popular playwright.[3] Finally, on February 18, he left a card for Wilde at his club. The card read: "For Oscar Wilde posing Somdomite [sic]."[4] Urged on by Douglas, Wilde sued for libel. When he lost the libel suit, Wilde was accordingly tried under the Labouchere Amendment for committing "acts of gross indecency."[5] Strikingly, the prosecution turned to Wilde's writings to confirm his alleged depravity, putting *The Picture of Dorian Gray* forth as a "sodomitical novel."[6] Wilde refused to accept the classification offered by prosecutor Edward Carson:

---

1   Wilde, *The Picture of Dorian Gray* 210.

2   Merlin Holland, ed., *The Real Trial of Oscar Wilde* (New York: Harper Collins, 2003), 58.

3   Holland 36.

4   Holland 4.

5   Also known as the Criminal Law Amendment Act of 1885, the Labouchere Amendment criminalized "gross indecency" without offering any specific definition of the term. Until 1861, the penalty for sodomy had been death. The severity of this sentence and the difficulty of providing clear evidence made such acts difficult to prosecute. The capacious term "gross indecency," combined with the introduction of imprisonment as a sentence, made it far easier to prosecute a range of homosexual behaviors.

6   Holland 81.

CARSON: May I take it that no matter how immoral a book was, if it was well written it would be a good book?

WILDE: If it were well written it would produce a sense of beauty, which is the highest feeling that man is capable of. If it was badly written it would produce a sense of disgust.

CARSON: A well written, immoral book would—

WILDE: I beg your pardon—I say if a book is well written, that is if a work of art is beautiful, the impression that it produces is a sense of beauty, which is the very highest sense that I think human beings are capable of. If it is a badly made work of art, whether it be a statue or whether it be a book, it produces a sense of disgust; that is all.[1]

True to his aesthetic principles, Wilde insisted throughout the trial that his work did not seek to assert any particular view, instead presenting ideas and impressions that would provoke thought and even dissent. It was precisely the same objective he had adopted in *Salome*, and he was once again in the position of defending his work on the grounds that it promoted vice. To apply moral standards to art was to degrade and vulgarize it, limiting art's capacity to promote a process of free and natural inquiry. In effect, it was to imprison art within the artificial and restrictive walls of cultural convention.

Wilde was convicted and sentenced to two years of hard labor. During his term in Reading Gaol, he wrote regularly to Robert Ross, requesting long lists of books that included works by Flaubert (*La Tentation de Saint Antoine, Trois Contes, Salammbô*), Pierre Louÿs's *Aphrodite*, Maeterlinck's works, a French Bible, reviews of *Salome*, and the play itself. While surrounded by prison walls, Wilde surrounded himself, that is to say, with precisely those works that had informed the composition of *Salome*. He had good reason to be thinking of the play at this time: the first production of *Salome* finally took place in Paris at the Théâtre de L'Oeuvre during his incarceration. For Wilde, news of the production was a rare comfort and helped partially to repair his damaged literary reputation. He notes in a letter written in June 1897: "The production of *Salomé* was the thing that turned the scale in my favour, as far as my treatment in prison by the Government was concerned, and I am deeply grateful to all concerned in it."[2] Given that Wilde was convicted for practicing what

1 Ibid.
2 Wilde, *Complete Letters* 872.

Lord Alfred Douglas famously described as "the love that dare not speak its name," it is striking that Wilde's imagination lingered on *Salome*, a play that directly addressed the ineffable desires that underlie everyday experience.

Suggestively, the production history of *Salome* has repeatedly called attention to this tension between art and cultural politics, from the multiracial productions of the Harlem Renaissance and the spectacularly sexualized 1923 silent film starring Alla Nazimova, to Rita Hayworth's 1953 portrayal of Salome as ingénue and Ken Russell's campy 1988 film *Salome's Last Dance*.[1] The most noteworthy case is perhaps that of Maud Allan, who became renowned for her performance of "A Vision of Salome" in 1906. Just as Wilde's writing was used as evidence against him during the 1895 trial, so too was Allan asked to justify her performance of Salome in the courtroom. In 1918, Noel Pemberton Billington published an article in his paper, then called *The Imperialist*, alleging the existence of a "Black Book" containing the names of 47,000 British citizens, sexual "deviants" who were being blackmailed by the German government. Later, the paper (now known as *The Vigilante*) claimed that an "Unseen Hand" consisting of sexually deviant German agents was infesting the country with venereal disease and deviant behavior. Finally, Billington published a short notice insinuating that Maud Allan was complicit in this strange conspiracy (Appendix E14, pp. 145-46). In response to "The Cult of the Clitoris," Allan sued Billington for libel. The suit, unlike Wilde's, was ultimately successful. During the trial, Billington undertook his own defense and, determined to demonstrate Allan's proclivity for sexual perversion, requested that she interpret select passages from Wilde's play and called upon Douglas himself to confirm the play's ostensibly salacious undertones (Appendix E15). Throughout, Allan insisted that the play was anything but perverted: "Salome fell in love with the holiness and the beauty of this man [Iokanaan] ... And she feels the insult of this man who treats her as a wanton and a harlot, which she was not."[2] In her defense of *Salome*, Allan stressed that far from being a play about incestuous lust, deviant

---

1 For a discussion of Harlem Renaissance productions of *Salome*, see Margaux Poueymirou, "The Race to Perform: *Salome* and the Wilde Harlem Renaissance," in Bennett 201-19.

2 Verbatim Report of the Trial of Noel Pemberton Billington, MP on a Charge of Criminal Libel (London: Vigilante Office, 1918), 103. For an insightful account of the trial, see Michael Kettle, *Salome's Last Veil: The Libel Case of the Century* (London: Granada Publishing, 1977).

longing, and religious transgression, the character of Salome was herself a reflection of laudable desire who "admires what is beautiful and [...] hates everything that is coarse and vulgar" (Appendix E15, p. 147). In other words, Allan defended her own artistry and Wilde's in the same breath by arguing that the play's reimagining of Scripture reflects an attempt to understand art as a mediator between this world and the next. Wilde could not have said it better himself.

Oscar Wilde: A Brief Chronology

1854 16 October, Oscar Fingal O'Flahertie Wills Wilde born in Dublin to ophthalmologist Sir William Wilde and writer Jane Francesca ("Speranza") Wilde.

1864 Attends the Portora Royal School, Enniskillen.

1871 Continues his studies at Trinity College, Dublin.

1874 Matriculates at Magdalen College, Oxford.

1881 *Poems* published; helps to establish Wilde's reputation as an aesthete.

1882 Commences a lecture tour of North America. At the time, Gilbert and Sullivan's *Patience*, an opera lampooning the aesthetes, is playing at the Standard Theatre, New York.

1884 Marries Constance Lloyd.

1885 A son, Cyril, is born. The Labouchere Amendment criminalizes acts of "gross indecency."

1886 Second son, Vyvyan, is born.

1887 Begins editing *Woman's World*, a post he will hold until 1889.

1888 *The Happy Prince and Other Tales* published.

1889 "The Portrait of Mr. W.H." published in *Blackwood's Magazine*. "The Decay of Lying" published in *The Nineteenth Century*.

1890 *The Picture of Dorian Gray* serialized in *Lippincott's Magazine*.

1891 *The Picture of Dorian Gray* published as a book. *Intentions, Lord Arthur Savile's Crime and Other Stories*, and *A House of Pomegranates* published. Meets Lord Alfred ("Bosie") Douglas in January. In October, mentions to Wilfrid Scawen Blunt that he is "writing a play in French to be acted in the Français."[1] At the end of the month, leaves for Paris, where he meets Marcel Proust, Pierre Louÿs, André Gide, Stéphane Mallarmé, and others. Completes *Salome* by the end of November in Torquay.

1892 *Lady Windermere's Fan* produced at the St. James's Theatre. Writes *A Woman of No Importance*. In May, reads *Salome* to Sarah Bernhardt at the home of Henry Irving. In June, mentions to Pierre Louÿs that rehearsals of *Salome* are taking place at the Palace Theatre and that

---

1 Wilde, *Complete Letters* 506n1.

Bernhardt will play the title role. Later that month, the play is banned by the Lord Chamberlain.

1893   *Lady Windermere's Fan* and *A Woman of No Importance* published. The original French edition of *Salome* published in London and Paris. In August, Douglas begins translating the play into English.

1894   The first English translation of *Salome* published, accompanied by Aubrey Beardsley's illustrations. Writes *The Importance of Being Earnest*.

1895   *An Ideal Husband* performed at the Haymarket Theatre and *The Importance of Being Earnest* produced at the St. James's Theatre. Douglas's father, the Marquess of Queensberry, leaves his card for Wilde at the Albemarle Club with an inscription: "To Oscar Wilde posing Somdomite [*sic*]." Wilde brings libel suit against Queensberry and loses. As a result, Wilde himself is charged with acts of "gross indecency" and sentenced to two years of hard labor.

1896   First performance of *Salome* takes place on 11 February at the Théâtre de L'Oeuvre, Paris.

1897   In prison, writes a letter to Douglas that will later be published as *De Profundis*.

1898   *The Ballad of Reading Gaol* published. Constance Wilde dies following an unsuccessful surgery to address spinal paralysis (initially brought on by a bad fall in 1895). Aubrey Beardsley dies of tuberculosis.

1900   30 November, Wilde dies of cerebral meningitis at the Hotel D'Alsace, Paris.

1902   Max Reinhardt produces *Salome* at the Kleines Theater, Berlin. Richard Strauss and Maud Allan attend performances.

1905   A private performance of *Salome* is produced at the Bijou Theatre, London. *Salome* is produced at the Berkeley Lyceum, New York. Richard Strauss's *Salome* premieres in Dresden.

1906   *Salome* is staged privately, along with *A Florentine Tragedy*, by the Literary Theatre Society at King's Hall, Covent Garden. Maud Allan's "Vision of Salome" premieres in Vienna.

1931   Nancy Price produces the first public performance of *Salome* at the Savoy Theatre, London.

A Note on the Text

Salome was produced at an especially vibrant period of Wilde's career. In 1891, the year he began composing the play, he wrote his first successful drama, *Lady Windermere's Fan*. He also published *The Picture of Dorian Gray* as a book, along with a volume of criticism (*Intentions*), a collection of short fiction (*Lord Arthur Savile's Crime and Other Stories*), and a book of fairy tales (*A House of Pomegranates*). Wilde's ability to work across genres reflects his incredible versatility as a writer, and this proclivity for experimentation is perhaps nowhere better expressed than in *Salome*.

The greatest challenge to an editor of *Salome* stems from the fact that the text was written in French by an Irish playwright. The three existing manuscripts of *Salome* were produced between October 1891 and January 1892. They are housed at the Bodmer Library (Geneva), University of Texas (Austin), and the Rosenbach Museum (Philadelphia). Written in French, these manuscripts bear the marginalia of three French Symbolist poets: Alfred Retté, Pierre Louÿs, and the American-born Stuart Merrill. Wilde had requested that these acquaintances review the manuscript and help to refine, as Retté puts it, "those anglicisms which are too explicit."[1] The responses were varied. Retté admired the manuscript on the whole. Merrill reportedly observed "a certain perceived awkwardness" in Wilde's French, yet observed that "it's precisely the exotic nature of Wilde's French which seems to me to be one of the attractions of the play."[2] He noted additionally: "Salome was written in French by Wilde, then revised and corrected by me, Retté and Pierre Louÿs, in that order, but solely from the point of view of the language. Marcel Schwob corrected the proofs. Wilde was thus the sole author of *Salome*, any corrections that were made being only for the purpose of drawing attention to the faults in his French."[3] Although the collaborative editing of *Salome* might seem to compromise Wilde's claim to ownership over the play, the corrections made by these hands were relatively minor, pertaining primarily to grammar and punctuation. As Wilde's literary executor, Robert Ross, notes, "no one who knew Oscar Wilde with any

---

1 Mikhail 190.
2 Ibid.
3 Mikhail 469.

degree of intimacy would admit that *Salomé*, whatever its faults or merits or deprivations, owed anything considerable to the invention or talents of others."[1]

The original French edition of *Salome* was published in 1893 by Elkin Matthews and John Lane. Cloaked in purple paper wrappers with silver lettering on the front, this edition consisted of 600 copies. The dedication read: "À mon ami Pierre Louÿs," thus paying tribute to his influence on earlier drafts of the play. In 1893, Lord Alfred Douglas commenced work on an English translation, to be accompanied by Aubrey Beardsley's illustrations. Although Wilde had admired Beardsley's work prior to the commission, he found the complete set of illustrations produced for *Salome* to be highly objectionable. In the end, the first English edition included Beardsley's illustrations, which have been consistently associated with the play ever since. Appendix B includes a selection of these illustrations in an attempt to highlight the tensions between the very different aesthetic visions of Wilde and Beardsley.

Douglas's translation also presented problems. Peppered with technical errors and modified at times by his own poetic vagaries, it was unacceptable to Wilde and led to a prolonged quarrel between the two men. In the end, Wilde himself corrected Douglas's translation. Douglas was not credited on the title page of the first English edition, which appeared (also to Wilde's dismay) in blue canvas boards stamped on either side with a design by Beardsley. Wilde did, however, offer a conciliatory gesture to Douglas in his dedication: "To my friend Lord Alfred Bruce Douglas the translator of this play."

Douglas's translation was republished in 1906, 1907, and 1912, though each of these editions included corrections by Robert Ross. Over the years, others have attempted to provide more faithful translations of the play, including Wilde's youngest son Vyvyan Holland (London: Folio Society, 1957), whose edition does not include Beardsley's illustrations; R.A. Walker (London: Heinemann, 1957), who curiously identifies Beardsley as the play's author on the cover; Richard Howard (1978), whose translation concludes with Salome's strangulation at the hands of the Executioner; Joseph Donohue (Virginia: U of Virginia P, 2011), who renders the text into contemporary American-English; and Richard Ellmann (1982).

This Broadview edition presents the translation of Lord Alfred Douglas, since this was the only English translation overseen and

---

1　Ross 3.

at least partially executed by Wilde himself. In the case of scriptural references, I have referred to the King James Bible, chiefly because Douglas himself draws upon it in his translation, though it is likely that Wilde consulted Lemaître de Sacy's seventeenth-century French translation of the Bible in producing the original play.[1] In order to account for discrepancies among various translations of the text, however, I have included in Appendix D a chart comparing the original French and select English editions of the text. Although the English text is presented here, the notes and accompanying materials frequently provide information related to the original French edition. Consequently, the spelling of the play's title varies depending on which edition is being discussed and occasionally on the personal preference of the individuals being cited. For quoted passages appearing in the introduction, notes, and appendices, I have preserved the spelling as it appears in the original source material. Otherwise, in the interest of consistency, I have reverted to the English spelling in all material authored by myself.

---

1 For an excellent discussion of Wilde's use of the de Sacy Bible, see Peter Cogman, "Translation, Tenses, and Progression in the Final Monologue of Wilde's *Salomé*," *Birth and Death in Nineteenth-Century French Culture*, ed. Nigel Harkness et al. (Amsterdam: Rodopi, 2007), 81-95.

SALOME

THE PERSONS OF THE PLAY

HEROD ANTIPAS,[1] TETRARCH[2] OF JUDEA

IOKANAAN,[3] THE PROPHET

THE YOUNG SYRIAN, CAPTAIN OF THE GUARD

TIGELLINUS, A YOUNG ROMAN[4]

A CAPPADOCIAN[5]

A NUBIAN[6]

FIRST SOLDIER

SECOND SOLDIER

THE PAGE OF HERODIAS

---

1 Herod Antipas married Herodias, his brother's wife. For this reason,
   Herod Antipas was maligned by John the Baptist, whom he later had
   decapitated (Matthew 6:14-29). Although identified explicitly as Herod
   Antipas in the dramatis personae, Wilde also incorporates into this character features of Herod the Great and Herod Agrippa. According to
   Robert Ross: "It has been remarked that Wilde confuses Herod the
   Great (Matt.xi.I), Herod Antipas (Matt.xiv.3) and Herod Agrippa (Acts.
   xiii), but the confusion is intentional, as in mediaeval mystery plays
   Herod is taken for a type, not an historical character, and the criticism is
   about as valuable as that of people who laboriously point out the
   anachronisms in Beardsley's designs for the play" (xvii-xviii).
2 Regional governor.
3 Hebrew designation for John the Baptist. Flaubert also used the name
   Iokanaan in "Hérodias" (1877) (Appendix A7, pp. 96-99).
4 Also the name of a prefect of the Praetorian Guard who served under
   Nero and was known for his cruelty.
5 Cappadocia was an ancient kingdom and early center of Christian
   thought, located in present-day Turkey.
6 Nubia was an ancient region of Africa and the site of Christian mission-
   ary work as early as the second century.

JEWS, NAZARENES, ETC.

A SLAVE

NAAMAN,[1] THE EXECUTIONER

HERODIAS, WIFE OF THE TETRARCH[2]

SALOME, DAUGHTER OF HERODIAS

THE SLAVES OF SALOME

1   The name of a captain in the Syrian army who, as recounted in 2 Kings,
    was cured of leprosy by submerging himself seven times in the Jordan
    River. His story is often invoked as a forerunner to the ritual of Chris-
    tian baptism.
2   A Jewish Princess whose first marriage to her uncle, Herod II (some-
    times called Herod Philip I), produced Salome. Her second marriage
    was to Herod Antipas.

SALOME

SCENE—A great terrace in the Palace of Herod, set above the banqueting-hall. Some soldiers are leaning over the balcony. To the right there is a gigantic staircase, to the left, at the back, an old cistern[1] surrounded by a wall of green bronze. The moon is shining very brightly.

THE YOUNG SYRIAN. How beautiful is the Princess Salome tonight![2]

THE PAGE OF HERODIAS. Look at the moon. How strange the moon seems! She is like a woman rising from a tomb. She is like a dead woman. One might fancy she was looking for dead things.

THE YOUNG SYRIAN. She has a strange look. She is like a little princess who wears a yellow veil, and whose feet are of silver. She is like a princess who has little white doves for feet. One might fancy she was dancing.[3]

THE PAGE OF HERODIAS. She is like a woman who is dead. She moves very slowly.

[Noise in the banqueting-hall.]

FIRST SOLDIER. What an uproar! Who are those wild beasts howling?

---

1   A waterproof vessel designed to collect rainwater.
2   Wilde used this line in the inscription to Sarah Bernhardt's copy of the fifth edition of *Poems* (1881), preserving the original French: "À Sarah Bernhardt, 'Comme la Princesse Salomé est belle ce soir'" (*Complete Letters* 529n1).
3   In "The Fisherman and His Soul," Wilde compares a fisherman's encounter with lust to the figure of a dancing girl: "[...] a girl whose face was veiled ran in and began to dance before us. Her face was veiled with a veil of gauze, but her feet were naked. Naked were her feet, and they move over the carpet like little white pigeons. Never have I seen anything so marvelous [...]" (192). Oscar Wilde, "The Fisherman and His Soul," *The Complete Short Stories* (New York: Oxford UP, 2010), 171-201.

SECOND SOLDIER. The Jews. They are always like that. They are disputing about their religion.

FIRST SOLDIER. Why do they dispute about their religion?

SECOND SOLDIER. I cannot tell. They are always doing it. The Pharisees,[1] for instance, say that there are angels, and the Sadducees[2] declare that angels do not exist.

FIRST SOLDIER. I think it is ridiculous to dispute about such things.

THE YOUNG SYRIAN. How beautiful is the Princess Salome tonight!

THE PAGE OF HERODIAS. You are always looking at her. You look at her too much. It is dangerous to look at people in such fashion. Something terrible may happen.

THE YOUNG SYRIAN. She is very beautiful tonight.

FIRST SOLDIER. The Tetrarch has a sombre aspect.

SECOND SOLDIER. Yes; he has a sombre aspect.

FIRST SOLDIER. He is looking at something.

SECOND SOLDIER. He is looking at some one.

FIRST SOLDIER. At whom is he looking?

SECOND SOLDIER. I cannot tell.

THE YOUNG SYRIAN. How pale the Princess is! Never have I seen her so pale. She is like the shadow of a white rose in a mirror of silver.[3]

THE PAGE OF HERODIAS. You must not look at her. You look too much at her.

1　A Jewish sect distinguished by its belief in the Oral Law, the idea that God bestowed upon Moses both the Torah and an unwritten set of edicts illuminating the meaning of the Torah. The Oral law, after being transmitted by the followers of Moses over several generations, would eventually be recorded in the Talmud. The Pharisees stressed the importance of understanding the spirit of the Torah through textual interpretation and reflection.

2　In contrast to the Pharisees, the Sadducees rejected belief in the Oral Law and promoted the literal interpretation of Scripture.

3　In *The Picture of Dorian Gray*, Wilde describes the doomed actress Sibyl Vane as blushing "like the shadow of a rose in a mirror of silver" (302). Wilde also refers to a "red rose in a mirror of silver" (82) in his short

FIRST SOLDIER. Herodias has filled the cup of the Tetrarch.

THE CAPPADOCIAN. Is that the Queen Herodias, she who wears a black mitre sewed with pearls, and whose hair is powdered with blue dust?

FIRST SOLDIER. Yes; that is Herodias, the Tetrarch's wife.

SECOND SOLDIER. The Tetrarch is very fond of wine. He has wine of three sorts. One which is brought from the Island of Samothrace,[1] and is purple like the cloak of Cæsar.

THE CAPPADOCIAN. I have never seen Cæsar.

SECOND SOLDIER. Another that comes from a town called Cyprus,[2] and is as yellow as gold.

THE CAPPADOCIAN. I love gold.

SECOND SOLDIER. And the third is a wine of Sicily.[3] That wine is as red as blood.

THE NUBIAN. The gods of my country are very fond of blood. Twice in the year we sacrifice to them young men and maidens; fifty young men and a hundred maidens. But I am afraid that we never give them quite enough, for they are very harsh to us.

THE CAPPADOCIAN. In my country there are no gods left. The Romans have driven them out. There are some who say that they have hidden themselves in the mountains, but I do not believe it. Three nights I have been on the mountains

---

story "The Nightingale and the Rose" (Oscar Wilde, "The Nightingale and the Rose," *The Complete Short Stories*, 79-84). Elsewhere, the silver mirror relates to the act of interpreting art. In "The Critic as Artist," Wilde notes that the true critic of art "will prefer to look into the silver mirror or through the woven veil, and will turn his eyes away from the chaos and clamour of actual existence, though the mirror be tarnished and the veil be torn. His sole aim is to chronicle his own impressions" (262).

1 A Greek island located in the north Aegean Sea. Historically, Samothrace was also the location of the Sanctuary of the Great Gods, home of an important Pan-Hellenic religious cult.

2 An island in the Mediterranean Sea. It is sometimes thought to have been the birthplace of Aphrodite, Greek goddess of pleasure, beauty, and love.

3 An island in the Mediterranean Sea. It was presumably here that Persephone (daughter of the Greek god Zeus and the harvest goddess Demeter) was abducted by Hades, king of the underworld.

seeking them everywhere. I did not find them. And at last I called them by their names, and they did not come. I think they are dead.

FIRST SOLDIER. The Jews worship a God that one cannot see.[1]

THE CAPPADOCIAN. I cannot understand that.

FIRST SOLDIER. In fact, they only believe in things that one cannot see.

THE CAPPADOCIAN. That seems to me altogether ridiculous.

THE VOICE OF IOKANAAN. After me shall come another mightier than I. I am not worthy so much as to unloose the latchet of his shoes. When he cometh, the solitary places shall be glad. They shall blossom like the rose. The eyes of the blind shall see the day, and the ears of the deaf shall be opened.[2] The sucking child shall put his hand upon the dragon's lair, he shall lead lions by their manes.[3]

SECOND SOLDIER. Make him be silent. He is always saying ridiculous things.

FIRST SOLDIER. No, no. He is a holy man. He is very gentle, too. Every day, when I give him to eat he thanks me.

THE CAPPADOCIAN. Who is he?

FIRST SOLDIER. A prophet.

THE CAPPADOCIAN. What is his name?

FIRST SOLDIER. Iokanaan.

THE CAPPADOCIAN. Whence comes he?

FIRST SOLDIER. From the desert, where he fed on locusts and wild honey. He was clothed in camel's hair, and round his loins he had a leathern belt.[4] He was very terrible to look

---

1 Exodus 33:20: "And he said, Thou canst not see my face: for there shall no man see me, and live."

2 Isaiah 35:5: "Then the eyes of the blind shall be opened, and the ears of the deaf shall be unstopped."

3 Isaiah 11:6: "The wolf also shall dwell with the lamb, and the leopard shall lie down with the kid; and the calf and the young lion and the fatling together; and a little child shall lead them."

4 Mark 1:6: "And John was clothed with camel's hair, and with a girdle of a skin about his loins; and he did eat locusts and wild honey"; Matthew

upon. A great multitude used to follow him. He even had disciples.

THE CAPPADOCIAN. What is he talking of?

FIRST SOLDIER. We can never tell. Sometimes he says things that affright one, but it is impossible to understand what he says.

THE CAPPADOCIAN. May one see him?

FIRST SOLDIER. No. The Tetrarch has forbidden it.

THE YOUNG SYRIAN. The Princess has hidden her face behind her fan! Her little white hands are fluttering like doves that fly to their dovecots. They are like white butterflies. They are just like white butterflies.

THE PAGE OF HERODIAS. What is that to you? Why do you look at her?

You must not look at her.... Something terrible may happen.

THE CAPPADOCIAN. [*pointing to the cistern.*] What a strange prison!

SECOND SOLDIER. It is an old cistern.

THE CAPPADOCIAN. An old cistern! That must be a poisonous place in which to dwell!

SECOND SOLDIER. Oh, no! For instance, the Tetrarch's brother, his elder brother, the first husband of Herodias the Queen, was imprisoned there for twelve years. It did not kill him. At the end of the twelve years he had to be strangled.[1]

THE CAPPADOCIAN. Strangled? Who dared to do that?

SECOND SOLDIER. [*pointing to the executioner, a huge negro.*] That man yonder, Naaman.

THE CAPPADOCIAN. He was not afraid?

SECOND SOLDIER. Oh no! The Tetrarch sent him the ring.

3:4: "And the same John had his raiment of camel's hair, and a leathern girdle about his loins; and his meat was locusts and wild honey."

1 The only account of his death was recorded by Flavius Josephus in *Antiquities* (c. 94): "ABOUT this time it was that Philip, king of Macedon, was treacherously assaulted and slain at Egae by Pausanias, the son of Cerastes, who was derived from the family of Oreste, and his son Alexander succeeded him in the kingdom." Flavius Josephus, *Antiquities of the Jews* (London: Wordsworth Editions, 2006), 479.

THE CAPPADOCIAN. What ring?

SECOND SOLDIER. The death-ring. So he was not afraid.

THE CAPPADOCIAN. Yet it is a terrible thing to strangle a king.

FIRST SOLDIER. Why? Kings have but one neck, like other folk.

THE CAPPADOCIAN. I think it terrible.

THE YOUNG SYRIAN. The Princess is getting up! She is leaving the table! She looks very troubled. Ah, she is coming this way. Yes, she is coming towards us. How pale she is! Never have I seen her so pale.

THE PAGE OF HERODIAS. Do not look at her. I pray you not to look at her.

THE YOUNG SYRIAN. She is like a dove that has strayed.... She is like a narcissus trembling in the wind.... She is like a silver flower.

[Enter Salome.]

SALOME. I will not stay. I cannot stay. Why does the Tetrarch look at me all the while with his mole's eyes under his shaking eyelids? It is strange that the husband of my mother looks at me like that. I know not what it means. Of a truth I know it too well.

THE YOUNG SYRIAN. You have left the feast, Princess?

SALOME. How sweet is the air here! I can breathe here! Within there are Jews from Jerusalem who are tearing each other in pieces over their foolish ceremonies, and barbarians who drink and drink, and spill their wine on the pavement, and Greeks from Smyrna with painted eyes and painted cheeks, and frizzed hair curled in columns, and Egyptians silent and subtle, with long nails of jade and russet cloaks, and Romans brutal and coarse, with their uncouth jargon. Ah! how I loathe the Romans! They are rough and common, and they give themselves the airs of noble lords.

THE YOUNG SYRIAN. Will you be seated, Princess?

THE PAGE OF HERODIAS. Why do you speak to her? Oh! something terrible will happen. Why do you look at her?

SALOME. How good to see the moon! She is like a little piece of money, a little silver flower. She is cold and chaste. I am sure she is a virgin. She has the beauty of a virgin. Yes, she is a virgin. She has never defiled herself. She has never abandoned herself to men, like the other goddesses.[1]

THE VOICE OF IOKANAAN. Behold! the Lord hath come. The Son of Man is at hand.[2] The centaurs[3] have hidden themselves in the rivers, and the nymphs[4] have left the rivers, and are lying beneath the leaves in the forests.

SALOME. Who was that who cried out?

SECOND SOLDIER. The prophet, Princess.

SALOME. Ah, the prophet! He of whom the Tetrarch is afraid?

SECOND SOLDIER. We know nothing of that, Princess. It was the prophet Iokanaan who cried out.

THE YOUNG SYRIAN. Is it your pleasure that I bid them bring your litter,[5] Princess? The night is fair in the garden.

SALOME. He says terrible things about my mother, does he not?

SECOND SOLDIER. We never understand what he says, Princess.

SALOME. Yes; he says terrible things about her.

[*Enter a Slave.*]

---

1 Salome refers to the tradition of Greek and Roman mythology, which prominently features gods and goddesses who have sexual relations with human beings.

2 Refers to the coming of the Messiah. Matthew 25:31: "When the Son of man shall come in his glory, and all the holy angels with him, then shall he sit upon the throne of his glory."

3 In Greek mythology, a hybrid being that is part human and part horse. The centaur was thought to be a sexually potent and seductive creature.

4 In Greek mythology, divine spirits who pervade and animate nature. Typically young, beautiful, and amorous, nymphs are neither goddesses nor human beings.

5 A portable and sometimes curtained couch mounted upon poles and carried by servants or animals. A litter is typically meant to accommodate an eminent person.

THE SLAVE. Princess, the Tetrarch prays you to return to the feast.

SALOME. I will not return.

THE YOUNG SYRIAN. Pardon me, Princess, but if you return not some misfortune may happen.

SALOME. Is he an old man, this prophet?

THE YOUNG SYRIAN. Princess, it were better to return. Suffer me to lead you in.

SALOME. This prophet ... is he an old man?

FIRST SOLDIER. No, Princess, he is quite young.

SECOND SOLDIER. One cannot be sure. There are those who say that he is Elias.[1]

SALOME. Who is Elias?

SECOND SOLDIER. A prophet of this country in bygone days, Princess.

THE SLAVE. What answer may I give the Tetrarch from the Princess?

THE VOICE OF IOKANAAN. Rejoice not, O land of Palestine, because the rod of him who smote thee is broken. For from the seed of the serpent shall come a basilisk, and that which is born of it shall devour the birds.[2]

SALOME. What a strange voice! I would speak with him.

FIRST SOLDIER. I fear it may not be, Princess. The Tetrarch does not suffer any one to speak with him. He has even forbidden the high priest to speak with him.

SALOME. I desire to speak with him.

FIRST SOLDIER. It is impossible, Princess.

SALOME. I will speak with him.

---

1 The passage seems to refer to Christ in a passage from Mark that invokes John the Baptist and immediately precedes the story of his beheading. Mark 6:15-16: "Others said, That it is Elias. And others said, That it is a prophet, or as one of the prophets. / But when Herod heard *thereof*, he said, It is John, whom I beheaded: he is risen from the dead."
2 Isaiah 14:29: "Rejoice not thou, whole Palestina, because the rod of him that smote thee is broken: for out of the serpent's root shall come forth a cockatrice, and his fruit *shall* be a fiery flying serpent."

THE YOUNG SYRIAN. Would it not be better to return to the banquet?

SALOME. Bring forth this prophet.

[*Exit the Slave.*]

FIRST SOLDIER. We dare not, Princess.

SALOME. [*approaching the cistern and looking down into it.*] How black it is down there! It must be terrible to be in so black a hole! It is like a tomb.... [*To the soldiers.*] Did you not hear me? Bring out the prophet. I would look on him.

SECOND SOLDIER. Princess, I beg you, do not require this of us.

SALOME. You are making me wait upon your pleasure.

FIRST SOLDIER. Princess, our lives belong to you, but we cannot do what you have asked of us. And indeed, it is not of us that you should ask this thing.

SALOME. [*looking at the young Syrian.*] Ah!

THE PAGE OF HERODIAS. Oh! what is going to happen? I am sure that something terrible will happen.

SALOME. [*going up to the young Syrian.*] Thou wilt do this thing for me, wilt thou not, Narraboth? Thou wilt do this thing for me. I have ever been kind towards thee. Thou wilt do it for me. I would but look at him, this strange prophet. Men have talked so much of him. Often I have heard the Tetrarch talk of him. I think he is afraid of him, the Tetrarch. Art thou, even thou, also afraid of him, Narraboth?

THE YOUNG SYRIAN. I fear him not, Princess; there is no man I fear. But the Tetrarch has formally forbidden that any man should raise the cover of this well.

SALOME. Thou wilt do this thing for me, Narraboth, and tomorrow when I pass in my litter beneath the gateway of the idol sellers I will let fall for thee a little flower, a little green flower.[1]

---

1 Wilde and his disciples were noted for wearing green carnations in their buttonholes, an ornament meant to reflect art's ability to transform everyday experience. The buttonhole was so closely aligned with Wilde and his followers that it became the title of Robert Hichens's 1894 roman à clef, *The Green Carnation*.

THE YOUNG SYRIAN. Princess, I cannot, I cannot.

SALOME. [*smiling.*] Thou wilt do this thing for me, Narraboth. Thou knowest that thou wilt do this thing for me. And on the morrow when I shall pass in my litter by the bridge of the idol-buyers, I will look at thee through the muslin veils, I will look at thee, Narraboth, it may be I will smile at thee. Look at me, Narraboth, look at me. Ah! thou knowest that thou wilt do what I ask of thee. Thou knowest it.... I know that thou wilt do this thing.

THE YOUNG SYRIAN. [*signing to the third Soldier.*] Let the prophet come forth.... The Princess Salome desires to see him.

SALOME. Ah!

THE PAGE OF HERODIAS. Oh! How strange the moon looks! Like the hand of a dead woman who is seeking to cover herself with a shroud.

THE YOUNG SYRIAN. She has a strange aspect! She is like a little princess, whose eyes are eyes of amber. Through the clouds of muslin she is smiling like a little princess.

[*The prophet comes out of the cistern. Salome looks at him and steps slowly back.*]

IOKANAAN. Where is he whose cup of abominations is now full?[1] Where is he, who in a robe of silver shall one day die in the face of all the people? Bid him come forth, that he may hear the voice of him who hath cried in the waste places and in the houses of kings.[2]

SALOME. Of whom is he speaking?

THE YOUNG SYRIAN. No one can tell, Princess.

---

1   Revelations 17:4-5: "And the woman was arrayed in purple and scarlet colour, and decked with gold and precious stones and pearls, having a golden cup in her hand full of abominations and filthiness of her fornication:/ And upon her forehead was a name written, MYSTERY, BABYLON THE GREAT, THE MOTHER OF HARLOTS AND ABOMINATIONS OF THE EARTH."

2   Another allusion to Elijah (Elias) who delivered prophecies in the desert as well as before kings. In 1 Kings 21, he prophesies that Jezebel will suffer a public death, which ultimately comes to pass in 2 Kings 9.

IOKANAAN. Where is she who saw the images of men painted on the walls, even the images of the Chaldæans painted with colours, and gave herself up unto the lust of her eyes, and sent ambassadors into the land of Chaldæa?[1]

SALOME. It is of my mother that he is speaking.

THE YOUNG SYRIAN. Oh no, Princess.

SALOME. Yes: it is of my mother that he is speaking.

IOKANAAN. Where is she who gave herself unto the Captains of Assyria, who have baldricks[2] on their loins, and crowns of many colours on their heads? Where is she who hath given herself to the young men of the Egyptians, who are clothed in fine linen and hyacinth, whose shields are of gold, whose helmets are of silver, whose bodies are mighty? Go, bid her rise up from the bed of her abominations, from the bed of her incestuousness, that she may hear the words of him who prepareth the way of the Lord, that she may repent her of her iniquities. Though she will not repent, but will stick fast in her abominations, go bid her come, for the fan of the Lord is in His hand.[3]

SALOME. Ah, but he is terrible, he is terrible!

THE YOUNG SYRIAN. Do not stay here, Princess, I beseech you.

SALOME. It is his eyes above all that are terrible. They are like black holes burned by torches in a tapestry of Tyre. They are

---

1 Alludes to the story of Aholibah, who in Ezekiel is punished for adultery, sexual license, and idolatry. The passage reflects the culmination of her sexual profligacy: "[...] for when she saw men pourtrayed upon the wall, the images of the Chaldeans pourtrayed with vermilion, / Girded with girdles upon their loins, exceeding in dyed attire upon their heads, all of them princes to look to, after the manner of the Babylonians of Chaldea, the land of their nativity: / And as soon as she saw them with her eyes, she doted upon them, and sent messengers unto them into Chaldea" (Ezekiel 23:14-16).

2 A belt, often used to carry a weapon.

3 In Matthew 3:11-12 and Luke 3:16-17, John the Baptist proclaims: "I indeed baptize you with water unto repentance: but he that cometh after me is mightier than I, whose shoes I am not worthy to bear: he shall baptize you with the Holy Ghost, and *with* fire: / Whose fan *is* in his hand, and he will thoroughly purge his floor, and gather his wheat into the garner; but he will burn up the chaff with unquenchable fire."

like the black caverns where the dragons live, the black caverns of Egypt in which the dragons make their lairs. They are like black lakes troubled by fantastic moons.... Do you think he will speak again?

THE YOUNG SYRIAN. Do not stay here, Princess. I pray you do not stay here.

SALOME. How wasted he is! He is like a thin ivory statue. He is like an image of silver. I am sure he is chaste, as the moon is. He is like a moonbeam, like a shaft of silver. His flesh must be very cold, cold as ivory.... I would look closer at him.

THE YOUNG SYRIAN. No, no, Princess!

SALOME. I must look at him closer.

THE YOUNG SYRIAN. Princess! Princess!

IOKANAAN. Who is this woman who is looking at me? I will not have her look at me. Wherefore doth she look at me, with her golden eyes, under her gilded eyelids? I know not who she is. I do not desire to know who she is. Bid her begone. It is not to her that I would speak.

SALOME. I am Salome, daughter of Herodias, Princess of Judæa.

IOKANAAN. Back! daughter of Babylon![1] Come not near the chosen of the Lord. Thy mother hath filled the earth with the wine of her iniquities, and the cry of her sinning hath come up even to the ears of God.[2]

---

1   The phrase appears several times in Scripture, yet one of the more relevant passages occurs in Isaiah 47:1-3: "Come down, and sit in the dust, O virgin daughter of Babylon, sit on the ground: *there is* no throne, O daughter of the Chaldeans: for thou shalt no more be called tender and delicate. / Take the millstones, and grind meal: uncover thy locks, make bare the leg, uncover the thigh, pass over the rivers. / Thy nakedness shall be uncovered, yea, thy shame shall be seen: I will take vengeance, and I will not meet *thee* as a man."

2   Images of wine-soaked earth frequently accompany allusions to fornication in Scripture, as the following two passages illustrate. Jeremiah 51:7: "Babylon *hath been* a golden cup in the LORD'S hand, that made all the earth drunken: the nations have drunken of her wine; therefore the nations are mad"; Revelation 17:2: "With whom the kings of the earth have committed fornication, and the inhabitants of the earth have been made drunk with the wine of her fornication."

SALOME. Speak again, Iokanaan. Thy voice is as music to mine ear.

THE YOUNG SYRIAN. Princess! Princess! Princess!

SALOME. Speak again! Speak again, Iokanaan, and tell me what I must do.

IOKANAAN. Daughter of Sodom,[1] come not near me! But cover thy face with a veil, and scatter ashes upon thine head, and get thee to the desert, and seek out the Son of Man.[2]

SALOME. Who is he, the Son of Man? Is he as beautiful as thou art, Iokanaan?

IOKANAAN. Get thee behind me! I hear in the palace the beating of the wings of the angel of death.

THE YOUNG SYRIAN. Princess, I beseech thee to go within.

IOKANAAN. Angel of the Lord God, what dost thou here with thy sword? Whom seekest thou in this palace? The day of him who shall die in a robe of silver has not yet come.[3]

SALOME. Iokanaan!

IOKANAAN. Who speaketh?

SALOME. I am amorous of thy body, Iokanaan! Thy body is white, like the lilies of a field that the mower hath never mowed.[4] Thy body is white like the snows that lie on the mountains of Judæa, and come down into the valleys. The roses in the garden of the Queen of Arabia are not so white as thy body. Neither the roses of the garden of the Queen of Arabia, the garden of spices of the Queen of Arabia, nor the feet of the dawn when they light on the leaves, nor the breast

---

1 Genesis 13:13: "But the men of Sodom were wicked and sinners before the LORD exceedingly."

2 Possibly a reference to Jeremiah's warning of impending evil: "O daughter of my people, gird *thee* with sackcloth, and wallow thyself in ashes: make thee mourning, *as for* an only son, most bitter lamentation: for the spoiler shall suddenly come upon us" (Jeremiah 6:26).

3 The color of Christ's robe has been variously described as purple (John 19:5), scarlet (Matthew 27:28), or simply "gorgeous" (Luke 23:11).

4 Matthew 6:27-29: "Which of you by taking thought can add one cubit unto his stature? / And why take ye thought for raiment? Consider the lilies of the field, how they grow; they toil not, neither do they spin: / And yet I say unto you, That even Solomon in all his glory was not arrayed like one of these."

of the moon when she lies on the breast of the sea.... There is nothing in the world so white as thy body. Suffer me to touch thy body.

IOKANAAN. Back! daughter of Babylon! By woman came evil into the world.[1] Speak not to me. I will not listen to thee. I listen but to the voice of the Lord God.

SALOME. Thy body is hideous. It is like the body of a leper. It is like a plastered wall, where vipers have crawled; like a plastered wall where the scorpions have made their nest. It is like a whited sepulchre, full of loathsome things. It is horrible, thy body is horrible. It is of thy hair that I am enamoured, Iokanaan. Thy hair is like clusters of grapes, like the clusters of black grapes that hang from the vine-trees of Edom in the land of the Edomites. Thy hair is like the cedars of Lebanon, like the great cedars of Labanon that gave their shade to the lions and to the robbers who would hide them by day.[2] The long black nights, when the moon hides her face, when the stars are afraid, are not so black as thy hair. The silence that dwells in the forest is not so black. There is nothing in the world that is so black as thy hair.... Suffer me to touch thy hair.

IOKANAAN. Back, daughter of Sodom! Touch me not. Profane not the temple of the Lord God.

SALOME. Thy hair is horrible. It is covered with mire and dust. It is like a crown of thorns placed on thy head.[3] It is like a knot of serpents coiled round thy neck. I love not thy

---

1 A reference to Genesis 3, in which, at the serpent's bidding, the first woman eats and invites the first man to eat of the tree of knowledge of good and evil.

2 Salome's address suggests strong parallels to the Song of Solomon, though here the comparisons are inverted, as in 5:10-15: "My beloved *is* white and ruddy, the chiefest among ten thousand. / His head *is* as the most fine gold, his locks *are* bushy, *and* black as a raven. / His eyes *are* as *the eyes* of doves by the rivers of waters, washed with milk, *and* fitly set. / His cheeks *are* as a bed of spices, *as* sweet flowers: his lips *like* lilies, dropping sweet smelling myrrh. / His hands *are as* gold rings set with the beryl: his belly *is as* bright ivory overlaid *with* sapphires. / His legs *are as* pillars of marble, set upon sockets of fine gold: his countenance *is* as Lebanon, excellent as the cedars."

3 Invokes the "crown of thorns" placed upon Christ's head in Mark 15:17, John 19:2, and Matthew 27:29.

hair.... It is thy mouth that I desire, Iokanaan. Thy mouth is like a band of scarlet on a tower of ivory. It is like a pomegranate cut in twain with a knife of ivory.[1] The pomegranate flowers that blossom in the gardens of Tyre, and are redder than roses, are not so red. The red blasts of trumpets that herald the approach of kings, and make afraid the enemy, are not so red. Thy mouth is redder than the feet of those who tread the wine in the wine-press. It is redder than the feet of the doves who inhabit the temples and are fed by the priests. It is redder than the feet of him who cometh from a forest where he hath slain a lion, and seen gilded tigers.[2] Thy mouth is like a branch of coral that fishers have found in the twilight of the sea, the coral that they keep for the kings! ... It is like the vermilion that the Moabites find in the mines of Moab, the vermilion that the kings take from them.[3] It is like the bow of the King of the Persians, that is painted with vermilion, and is tipped with coral. There is nothing in the world so red as thy mouth.... Suffer me to kiss thy mouth.

IOKANAAN. Never! daughter of Babylon! Daughter of Sodom! never!

SALOME. I will kiss thy mouth, Iokanaan. I will kiss thy mouth.

THE YOUNG SYRIAN. Princess, Princess, thou who art like a garden of myrrh, thou who art the dove of all doves, look not at this man, look not at him! Do not speak such words to him. I cannot endure it.... Princess, do not speak these things.

SALOME. I will kiss thy mouth, Iokanaan.

THE YOUNG SYRIAN. Ah!

---

1 Reflects the influence of Heinrich Heine's *Atta Troll* (1841-42), which describes Herodias as having "Soft lips, red like pomegranates" (Appendix A3, p. 90).

2 Possibly an allusion to Samson who, in Judges 14, slays a lion. Benaiah is also said to have slain a lion "in the midst of a pit in time of snow" (2 Samuel 23:20; also 1 Chronicles 11:22).

3 In 2 Kings 3, the prophet Elisha (Elijah) instructed the Israelites to defend themselves from the Moabites by digging ditches between themselves and their adversaries. At night, the ditches filled with water the color of blood. The Moabites, believing that the Israelites had slain one another, forged ahead and were defeated.

[*He kills himself, and falls between Salome and Iokanaan.*]

THE PAGE OF HERODIAS. The young Syrian has slain himself! The young captain has slain himself! He has slain himself who was my friend! I gave him a little box of perfumes and ear-rings wrought in silver, and now he has killed himself! Ah, did he not say that some misfortune would happen? I, too, said it, and it has come to pass. Well I knew that the moon was seeking a dead thing, but I knew not that it was he whom she sought. Ah! why did I not hide him from the moon? If I had hidden him in a cavern she would not have seen him.

FIRST SOLDIER. Princess, the young captain has just slain himself.

SALOME. Suffer me to kiss thy mouth, Iokanaan.

IOKANAAN. Art thou not afraid, daughter of Herodias? Did I not tell thee that I had heard in the palace the beating of the wings of the angel of death, and hath he not come, the angel of death?

SALOME. Suffer me to kiss thy mouth.

IOKANAAN. Daughter of adultery, there is but one who can save thee. It is He of whom I spake. Go seek Him. He is in a boat on the sea of Galilee, and He talketh with His disciples.[1] Kneel down on the shore of the sea, and call unto Him by His name. When He cometh to thee, and to all who call on Him He cometh, bow thyself at His feet and ask of Him the remission of thy sins.

SALOME. Suffer me to kiss thy mouth.

IOKANAAN. Cursed be thou! daughter of an incestuous mother, be thou accursed!

SALOME. I will kiss thy mouth, Iokanaan.

IOKANAAN. I will not look at thee. Thou art accursed, Salome, thou art accursed.

[*He goes down into the cistern.*]

---

1 In Matthew 4 and Mark 1, Christ begins to assemble disciples along the Sea of Galilee.

SALOME. I will kiss thy mouth, Iokanaan; I will kiss thy mouth.

FIRST SOLDIER. We must bear away the body to another place. The Tetrarch does not care to see dead bodies, save the bodies of those whom he himself has slain.

THE PAGE OF HERODIAS. He was my brother, and nearer to me than a brother. I gave him a little box full of perfumes, and a ring of agate that he wore always on his hand. In the evening we were wont to walk by the river, and among the almond-trees, and he used to tell me of the things of his country. He spake ever very low. The sound of his voice was like the sound of the flute, of one who playeth upon the flute.[1] Also, he had much joy to gaze at himself in the river.[2] I used to reproach him for that.

SECOND SOLDIER. You are right; we must hide the body. The Tetrarch must not see it.

FIRST SOLDIER. The Tetrarch will not come to this place. He never comes on the terrace. He is too much afraid of the prophet.

[*Enter Herod, Herodias, and all the Court: Tigellinus (Caesar's ambassador) and one other Roman, five Jews, two Nazarenes, three Slaves (Manasseh, Issachar, Ozias), and Salome's Slaves.*]

HEROD. Where is Salome? Where is the Princess? Why did she not return to the banquet as I commanded her? Ah! there she is!

HERODIAS. You must not look at her! You are always looking at her!

HEROD. The moon has a strange look tonight. Has she not a strange look? She is like a mad woman, a mad woman who is seeking everywhere for lovers. She is naked too. She is quite naked. The clouds are seeking to clothe her nakedness, but she will not let them. She shows herself naked in the sky. She

---

1 Perhaps an allusion to Pan, the nature god who in Greek mythology creates the first syrinx, or "pan pipes."

2 A reference to the Greek myth of Narcissus, a hunter renowned for his beauty. So great is his vanity that Narcissus is unable to stop looking at his own reflection in a pool of water and, in trying to kiss it, drowns.

reels through the clouds like a drunken woman.... I am sure she is looking for lovers. Does she not reel like a drunken woman? She is like a mad woman, is she not?

HERODIAS. No; the moon is like the moon, that is all. Let us go within.... We have nothing to do here.

HEROD. I will stay here! Manasseh, lay carpets there. Light torches. Bring forth the ivory tables, and the tables of jasper. The air here is sweet. I will drink more wine with my guests. We must show all honours to the ambassadors of Cæsar.

HERODIAS. It is not because of them that you remain.

HEROD. Yes; the air is very sweet. Come, Herodias, our guests await us. Ah! I have slipped! I have slipped in blood! It is an ill omen. It is a very ill omen. Wherefore is there blood here? ... and this body, what does this body here? Think you I am like the King of Egypt, who gives no feast to his guests but that he shows them a corpse? Whose is it? I will not look on it.

FIRST SOLDIER. It is our captain, sire. It is the young Syrian whom you made captain of the guard but three days gone.

HEROD. I issued no order that he should be slain.

SECOND SOLDIER. He slew himself, sire.

HEROD. For what reason? I had made him captain of my guard!

SECOND SOLDIER. We do not know, sire. But with his own hand he slew himself.

HEROD. That seems strange to me. I had thought it was but the Roman philosophers who slew themselves. Is it not true, Tigellinus, that the philosophers of Rome slay themselves?

TIGELLINUS. There be some who slay themselves, sire. They are the Stoics. The Stoics[1] are people of no cultivation. They are ridiculous people. I myself regard them as being perfectly ridiculous.

HEROD. I also. It is ridiculous to kill one's self.

---

1 Refers to the school of Greek philosophy, founded by Zeno in the fifth century BCE, that promoted the idea that negative emotions, such as fear or anger, result from errors in judgment. According to the Stoics, living a virtuous life and rejecting such emotions was the path to true wisdom and happiness.

TIGELLINUS. Everybody at Rome laughs at them. The Emperor has written a satire against them.[1] It is recited everywhere.

HEROD. Ah! he has written a satire against them? Cæsar is wonderful. He can do everything.... It is strange that the young Syrian has slain himself. I am sorry he has slain himself. I am very sorry. For he was fair to look upon. He was even very fair. He had very languorous eyes. I remember that I saw that he looked languorously at Salome. Truly, I thought he looked too much at her.

HERODIAS. There are others who look too much at her.

HEROD. His father was a king. I drave him from his kingdom. And of his mother who was a queen, you made a slave, Herodias. So he was here as my guest, as it were, and for that reason I made him my captain. I am sorry he is dead. Ho! why have you left the body here? It must be taken to some other place. I will not look at it,—away with it! [*They take away the body.*] It is cold here. There is a wind blowing. Is there not a wind blowing?

HERODIAS. No; there is no wind.

HEROD. I tell you there is a wind that blows.... And I hear in the air something that is like the beating of wings, like the beating of vast wings. Do you not hear it?

HERODIAS. I hear nothing.

HEROD. I hear it no longer. But I heard it. It was the blowing of the wind. It has passed away. But no, I hear it again. Do you not hear it? It is just like a beating of wings.

HERODIAS. I tell you there is nothing. You are ill. Let us go within.

HEROD. I am not ill. It is your daughter who is sick to death. Never have I see her so pale.

HERODIAS. I have told you not to look at her.

---

1   As in the case of Herod, Wilde draws upon several different emperors in his characterization of Caesar. Although Caesar Augustus is identified as the emperor in question, this may be an oblique reference to Nero, who fancied himself a literary figure and, though tutored by the Stoic philosopher Seneca, ultimately ordered his death by "forced suicide."

HEROD. Pour me forth wine. [*Wine is brought.*] Salome, come drink a little wine with me. I have here a wine that is exquisite. Cæsar himself sent it me. Dip into it thy little red lips, that I may drain the cup.

SALOME. I am not thirsty, Tetrarch.

HEROD. You hear how she answers me, this daughter of yours?

HERODIAS. She does right. Why are you always gazing at her?

HEROD. Bring me ripe fruits. [*Fruits are brought.*] Salome, come and eat fruits with me. I love to see in a fruit the mark of thy little teeth. Bite but a little of this fruit, that I may eat what is left.

SALOME. I am not hungry, Tetrarch.

HEROD. [*to Herodias.*] You see how you have brought up this daughter of yours.

HERODIAS. My daughter and I come of a royal race. As for thee, thy father was a camel driver! He was a thief and a robber to boot!

HEROD. Thou liest!

HERODIAS. Thou knowest well that it is true.

HEROD. Salome, come and sit next to me. I will give thee the throne of thy mother.

SALOME. I am not tired, Tetrarch.

HERODIAS. You see in what regard she holds you.

HEROD. Bring me—What is it that I desire? I forget. Ah! ah! I remember.

THE VOICE OF IOKANAAN. Behold the time is come! That which I foretold has come to pass. The day that I spake of is at hand.

HERODIAS. Bid him be silent. I will not listen to his voice. This man is for ever hurling insults against me.

HEROD. He has said nothing against you. Besides, he is a very great prophet.

HERODIAS. I do not believe in prophets. Can a man tell what will come to pass? No man knows it. Also he is for ever insulting me. But I think you are afraid of him.... I know well that you are afraid of him.

HEROD. I am not afraid of him. I am afraid of no man.

HERODIAS. I tell you, you are afraid of him. If you are not afraid of him why do you not deliver him to the Jews who for these six months past have been clamouring for him?

A JEW. Truly, my lord, it were better to deliver him into our hands.

HEROD. Enough on this subject. I have already given you my answer. I will not deliver him into your hands. He is a holy man. He is a man who has seen God.

A JEW. That cannot be. There is no man who hath seen God since the prophet Elias.[1] He is the last man who saw God face to face. In these days God doth not show Himself. God hideth Himself. Therefore great evils have come upon the land.

ANOTHER JEW. Verily, no man knoweth if Elias the prophet did indeed see God. Peradventure it was but the shadow of God that he saw.

A THIRD JEW. God is at no time hidden. He showeth Himself at all times and in all places. God is in what is evil even as He is in what is good.

A FOURTH JEW. Thou shouldst not say that. It is a very dangerous doctrine. It is a doctrine that cometh from Alexandria, where men teach the philosophy of the Greeks.[2] And the Greeks are Gentiles. They are not even circumcised.

---

1 John 1:21-23: "And they asked him, What then? Art thou Elias? And he saith, I am not. Art thou that prophet? And he answered, No. / Then said they unto him, Who art thou? That we may give an answer to them that sent us. What sayest thou of thyself? / He said, I *am* the voice of one crying in the wilderness, Make straight the way of the Lord, as said the prophet Esaias." See also Mark 6:14-16: "And king Herod heard of him; (for his name was spread abroad:) and he said, That John the Baptist was risen from the dead, and therefore mighty works do shew forth themselves in him. / Others said, That it is Elias. And others said, That it is a prophet, or as one of the prophets. / But when Herod heard thereof, he said, It is John, whom I beheaded: he is risen from the dead."

2 Possibly a reference to Gnosticism, which had strong roots in Alexandria. According to the Gnostics, the universe consists of both good and evil elements. The material world, which was thought by some to have been created by a lesser god or *demiurge*, is deeply flawed. Only through the pursuit of transcendent knowledge can one extract the good from this world and return it to its divine source.

A FIFTH JEW. No man can tell how God worketh. His ways are very dark. It may be that the things which we call evil are good, and that the things which we call good are evil.[1] There is no knowledge of anything. We can but bow our heads to His will, for God is very strong. He breaketh in pieces the strong together with the weak, for He regardeth not any man.

FIRST JEW. Thou speakest truly. Verily, God is terrible. He breaketh in pieces the strong and the weak as men break corn in a mortar. But as for this man, he hath never seen God. No man hath seen God since the prophet Elias.

HERODIAS. Make them be silent. They weary me.

HEROD. But I have heard it said that Iokanaan is in very truth your prophet Elias.

THE JEW. That cannot be. It is more than three hundred years since the days of the prophet Elias.

HEROD. There be some who say that this man is Elias the prophet.

A NAZARENE. I am sure that he is Elias the prophet.

THE JEW. Nay, but he is not Elias the prophet.

THE VOICE OF IOKANAAN. Behold the day is at hand, the day of the Lord, and I hear upon the mountains the feet of Him who shall be the Saviour of the world.

HEROD. What does that mean? The Saviour of the world?

TIGELLINUS. It is a title that Cæsar adopts.[2]

HEROD. But Cæsar is not coming into Judæa. Only yesterday I received letters from Rome. They contained nothing concerning this matter. And you, Tigellinus, who were at Rome during the winter, you heard nothing concerning this matter, did you?

TIGELLINUS. Sire, I heard nothing concerning the matter. I was but explaining the title. It is one of Cæsar's titles.

---

1   Isaiah 5:20: "Woe unto them that call evil good, and good evil; that put darkness for light, and light for darkness; that put bitter for sweet, and sweet for bitter!"

2   The rule of Caesar Augustus (27 BCE-14 CE) was characterized by peace. The *pax Augustus* led to his being widely acknowledged as "saviour of the world."

HEROD. But Cæsar cannot come. He is too gouty. They say that his feet are like the feet of an elephant. Also there are reasons of state. He who leaves Rome loses Rome. He will not come. Howbeit, Cæsar is lord, he will come if such be his pleasure. Nevertheless, I think he will not come.

FIRST NAZARENE. It was not concerning Cæsar that the prophet spake these words, sire.

HEROD. How?—it was not concerning Cæsar?

FIRST NAZARENE. No, my lord.

HEROD. Concerning whom then did he speak?

FIRST NAZARENE. Concerning Messias, who hath come.[1]

A JEW. Messias hath not come.

FIRST NAZARENE. He hath come, and everywhere He worketh miracles!

HERODIAS. Ho! ho! miracles! I do not believe in miracles. I have seen too many. [To the Page.] My fan.

FIRST NAZARENE. This Man worketh true miracles. Thus, at a marriage which took place in a little town of Galilee, a town of some importance, He changed water into wine.[2] Certain persons who were present related it to me. Also He healed two lepers that were seated before the Gate of Capernaum simply by touching them.[3]

SECOND NAZARENE. Nay; it was two blind men that He healed at Capernaum.[4]

FIRST NAZARENE. Nay; they were lepers. But He hath healed blind people also, and He was seen on a mountain talking with angels.[5]

A SADDUCEE. Angels do not exist.

A PHARISEE. Angels exist, but I do not believe that this Man has talked with them.

---

1 The Latin rendering of "messiah," which translates to "the anointed."

2 In John 2, Jesus turns water into wine at a wedding in Galilee.

3 Jesus cures lepers by touch in Matthew 8:1-4, Mark 1:40-45, and Luke 5:12-16.

4 Jesus heals two blind men in Matthew 9.

5 While Christ is often mentioned in connection with angels in the New Testament, it is Moses who speaks with the angel of God on Mount Sinai, prior to receiving the Ten Commandments.

FIRST NAZARENE. He was seen by a great multitude of people talking with angels.

HERODIAS. How these men weary me! They are ridiculous! They are altogether ridiculous! [*To the Page.*] Well! my fan? [*The Page gives her the fan.*] You have a dreamer's look. You must not dream. It is only sick people who dream. [*She strikes the Page with her fan.*]

SECOND NAZARENE. There is also the miracle of the daughter of Jairus.[1]

FIRST NAZARENE. Yea, that is sure. No man can gainsay it.

HERODIAS. Those men are mad. They have looked too long on the moon.[2] Command them to be silent.

HEROD. What is this miracle of the daughter of Jairus?

FIRST NAZARENE. The daughter of Jairus was dead. This Man raised her from the dead.

HEROD. How! He raises people from the dead?

FIRST NAZARENE. Yea, sire; He raiseth the dead.

HEROD. I do not wish Him to do that. I forbid Him to do that. I suffer no man to raise the dead. This Man must be found and told that I forbid Him to raise the dead. Where is this Man at present?

SECOND NAZARENE. He is in every place, my lord, but it is hard to find Him.

FIRST NAZARENE. It is said that He is now in Samaria.[3]

A JEW. It is easy to see that this is not Messias, if He is in Samaria. It is not to the Samaritans that Messias shall come. The Samaritans are accursed. They bring no offerings to the Temple.[4]

---

1 In the Gospels, Jairus tells Jesus that his daughter is dying, though she is in fact already dead. They return to the home of Jairus, where Jesus brings her back to life (Mark 5:21-43, Matthew 9:18-26, and Luke 8:40-56). Flaubert invokes the story as well in "Hérodias."

2 Reports of the lunar effect, the idea that changes in the moon cause madness, date back to the ancients.

3 In Luke 17:11-20, the place where Christ heals ten lepers.

4 The Samaritans maintained their own temple at Mount Gerizim, claiming that it (and not the temple at Jerusalem) was the true sanctuary for the people of Israel.

SECOND NAZARENE. He left Samaria a few days since. I think that at the present moment He is in the neighbourhood of Jerusalem.

FIRST NAZARENE. No; He is not there. I have just come from Jerusalem. For two months they have had no tidings of Him.

HEROD. No matter! But let them find Him, and tell Him, thus saith Herod the King, 'I will not suffer Thee to raise the dead.' To change water into wine, to heal the lepers and the blind.... He may do these things if He will. I say nothing against these things. In truth I hold it a kindly deed to heal a leper. But no man shall raise the dead.... It would be terrible if the dead came back.

THE VOICE OF IOKANAAN. Ah! The wanton one! The harlot! Ah! the daughter of Babylon with her golden eyes and her gilded eyelids! Thus saith the Lord God, Let there come up against her a multitude of men. Let the people take stones and stone her....

HERODIAS. Command him to be silent!

THE VOICE OF IOKANAAN. Let the captains of the hosts pierce her with their swords, let them crush her beneath their shields.

HERODIAS. Nay, but it is infamous.

THE VOICE OF IOKANAAN. It is thus that I will wipe out all wickedness from the earth, and that all women shall learn not to imitate her abominations.

HERODIAS. You hear what he says against me? You suffer him to revile her who is your wife!

HEROD. He did not speak your name.

HERODIAS. What does that matter? You know well that it is I whom he seeks to revile. And I am your wife, am I not?

HEROD. Of a truth, dear and noble Herodias, you are my wife, and before that you were the wife of my brother.

HERODIAS. It was thou didst snatch me from his arms.

HEROD. Of a truth I was stronger than he was.... But let us not talk of that matter. I do not desire to talk of it. It is the cause of the terrible words that the prophet has spoken. Peradventure on account of it a misfortune will come. Let us not speak of this matter. Noble Herodias, we are not mindful of our guests.

Fill thou my cup, my well-beloved. Ho! fill with wine the great goblets of silver, and the great goblets of glass. I will drink to Cæsar. There are Romans here, we must drink to Cæsar.

ALL. Cæsar! Cæsar!

HEROD. Do you not see your daughter, how pale she is?

HERODIAS. What is it to you if she be pale or not?

HEROD. Never have I see her so pale.

HERODIAS. You must not look at her.

THE VOICE OF IOKANAAN. In that day the sun shall become black like sackcloth of hair, and the moon shall become like blood, and the stars of the heaven shall fall upon the earth like unripe figs that fall from the fig-tree, and the kings of the earth shall be afraid.[1]

HERODIAS. Ah! ah! I should like to see that day of which he speaks, when the moon shall become like blood, and when the stars shall fall upon the earth like unripe figs. This prophet talks like a drunken man, ... but I cannot suffer the sound of his voice. I hate his voice. Command him to be silent.

HEROD. I will not. I cannot understand what it is that he saith, but it may be an omen.

HERODIAS. I do not believe in omens. He speaks like a drunken man.

HEROD. It may be he is drunk with the wine of God.

HERODIAS. What wine is that, the wine of God?[2] From what vineyards is it gathered? In what wine-press may one find it?[3]

---

1 Echoes the coming of the apocalypse in Revelations 6:12-13: "And I beheld when he had opened the sixth seal, and, lo, there was a great earthquake; and the sun became black as sackcloth of hair, and the moon became as blood; / And the stars of heaven fell unto the hearth, even as a fig tree casteth her untimely figs, when she is shaken of a mighty wind."

2 Revelations 14:9-10: "And the third angel followed them, saying with a loud voice, If any man worship the beast and his image, and receive his mark in his forehead, or in his hand, / The same shall drink of the wine of the wrath of God, which is poured out without mixture into the cup of his indignation; and he shall be tormented with fire and brimstone in the presence of the holy angels, and in the presence of the Lamb."

3 Revelations 14:19-20: "And the angel thrust in his sickle into the earth, and gathered the vine of the earth, and cast it into the great winepress of the wrath of God. / And the winepress was trodden without the city,

HEROD. [*from this point he looks all the while at Salome.*] Tigellinus, when you were at Rome of late, did the Emperor speak with you on the subject of ...?

TIGELLINUS. On what subject, my lord?

HEROD. On what subject? Ah! I asked you a question, did I not? I have forgotten what I would have asked you.

HERODIAS. You are looking again at my daughter. You must not look at her. I have already said so.

HEROD. You say nothing else.

HERODIAS. I say it again.

HEROD. And that restoration of the Temple about which they have talked so much, will anything be done?[1] They say that the veil of the sanctuary has disappeared, do they not?[2]

HERODIAS. It was thyself didst steal it. Thou speakest at random and without wit. I will not stay here. Let us go within.

HEROD. Dance for me, Salome.

HERODIAS. I will not have her dance.

SALOME. I have no desire to dance, Tetrarch.

HERODIAS. [*laughing.*] You see how she obeys you.

HEROD. What is it to me whether she dance or not? It is nought to me. Tonight I am happy. I am exceeding happy. Never have I been so happy.

FIRST SOLDIER. The Tetrarch has a sombre look. Has he not a sombre look?

SECOND SOLDIER. Yes, he has a sombre look.

---

and blood came out of the winepress, even unto the horse bridles, by the space of a thousand and six hundred furlongs."

1 The First Temple was built by King Solomon and destroyed by the Babylonians in 586 BCE. Herod the Great (as distinct from Herod Antipas, the character identified in Wilde's play) would oversee the construction of the Second Temple.

2 In the Holy Temple at Jerusalem, a veil concealed the "Holy of Holies," the inner sanctuary where the Ark of the Covenant was kept. According to the Gospels, the veil was torn when Christ died on the cross (Matthew 27:50-51, Mark 15:37-38, Luke 23:45-46). Later on, Herod offers Salome the veil of the sanctuary (p. 82).

HEROD. Wherefore should I not be happy? Cæsar, who is lord of the world, Cæsar, who is lord of all things, loves me well. He has just sent me most precious gifts. Also he has promised me to summon to Rome the King of Cappadocia, who is mine enemy.[1] It may be that at Rome he will crucify him, for he is able to do all things that he has a mind to do. Verily, Cæsar is lord. Therefore I do well to be happy. I am very happy, never have I been so happy. There is nothing in the world that can mar my happiness.

THE VOICE OF IOKANAAN. He shall be seated on his throne. He shall be clothed in scarlet and purple. In his hand he shall bear a golden cup full of his blasphemies. And the angel of the Lord shall smite him. He shall be eaten of worms.[2]

HERODIAS. You hear what he says about you. He says that you shall be eaten of worms.

HEROD. It is not of me that he speaks. He speaks never against me. It is of the King of Cappadocia that he speaks; the King of Cappadocia who is mine enemy. It is he who shall be eaten of worms. It is not I. Never has he spoken word against me, this prophet, save that I sinned in taking to wife the wife of my brother. It may be he is right. For, of a truth, you are sterile.

HERODIAS. I am sterile, I? You say that, you that are ever looking at my daughter, you that would have her dance for your pleasure? You speak as a fool. I have borne a child. You have gotten no child, no, not on one of your slaves. It is you who are sterile, not I.

---

1   According to Flavius Josephus, Herod the Great married his son, Alexander, to the daughter of Archelaus, then king of Cappadocia. Salome began a rumor that Alexander and his brother Aristobulus had consulted with Archelaus about charging Herod with the murder of their mother, Marianne, who had been executed for infidelity. By this account, the king of Cappadocia might be regarded anachronistically as complicit in a plot to undermine Herod's power.

2   Acts 12 describes Herod's meeting with the people of Tyre and Sidon, who have sought an audience with the king to request peace: "And upon a set day Herod, arrayed in royal apparel, sat upon his throne, and made an oration unto them. / And the people gave a shout, saying, It is the voice of a god, and not of a man. / And immediately the angel of the Lord smote him, because he gave not God the glory: and he was eaten of worms, and gave up the ghost" (Acts 12:21-23).

HEROD. Peace, woman! I say that you are sterile. You have borne me no child, and the prophet says that our marriage is not a true marriage. He says that it is a marriage of incest, a marriage that will bring evils.... I fear he is right; I am sure that he is right. But it is not the hour to speak of these things. I would be happy at this moment. Of a truth, I am happy. There is nothing I lack.

HERODIAS. I am glad you are of so fair a humour tonight. It is not your custom. But it is late. Let us go within. Do not forget that we hunt at sunrise. All honours must be shown to Cæsar's ambassadors, must they not?

SECOND SOLDIER. The Tetrarch has a sombre look.

FIRST SOLDIER. Yes, he has a sombre look.

HEROD. Salome, Salome, dance for me. I pray thee dance for me. I am sad to-night. Yes, I am passing sad tonight, when I came hither I slipped in blood, which is an ill omen; also I heard in the air a beating of wings, a beating of giant wings. I cannot tell what that may mean.... I am sad tonight. Therefore dance for me. Dance for me, Salome, I beseech thee. If thou dancest for me thou mayest ask of me what thou wilt, and I will give it thee. Yes, dance for me, Salome, and whatsoever thou shalt ask of me I will give it thee, even unto the half of my kingdom.

SALOME. [*rising.*] Will you indeed give me whatsoever I shall ask of you, Tetrarch?

HERODIAS. Do not dance, my daughter.

HEROD. Whatsoever thou shalt ask of me, even unto the half of my kingdom.

SALOME. You swear it, Tetrarch?

HEROD. I swear it, Salome.

HERODIAS. Do not dance, my daughter.

SALOME. By what will you swear this thing, Tetrarch?

HEROD. By my life, by my crown, by my gods. Whatsoever thou shalt desire I will give it thee, even to the half of my kingdom, if thou wilt but dance for me. O Salome, Salome, dance for me!

SALOME. You have sworn an oath, Tetrarch.

HEROD. I have sworn an oath.

HERODIAS. My daughter, do not dance.

HEROD. Even to the half of my kingdom. Thou wilt be passing fair as a queen, Salome, if it please thee to ask for the half of my kingdom. Will she not be fair as a queen? Ah! it is cold here! There is an icy wind, and I hear ... wherefore do I hear in the air this beating of wings? Ah! one might fancy a huge black bird that hovers over the terrace. Why can I not see it, this bird? The beat of its wings is terrible. The breath of the wind of its wings is terrible. It is a chill wind. Nay, but it is not cold, it is hot. I am choking. Pour water on my hands. Give me snow to eat. Loosen my mantle. Quick! quick! loosen my mantle. Nay, but leave it. It is my garland that hurts me, my garland of roses. The flowers are like fire. They have burned my forehead. [*He tears the wreath from his head, and throws it on the table.*] Ah! I can breathe now. How red those petals are! They are like stains of blood on the cloth. That does not matter. It is not wise to find symbols in everything that one sees. It makes life too full of terrors. It were better to say that stains of blood are as lovely as rose-petals. It were better far to say that.... But we will not speak of this. Now I am happy. I am passing happy. Have I not the right to be happy? Your daughter is going to dance for me. Wilt thou not dance for me, Salome? Thou hast promised to dance for me.

HERODIAS. I will not have her dance.

SALOME. I will dance for you, Tetrarch.

HEROD. You hear what your daughter says. She is going to dance for me. Thou doest well to dance for me, Salome. And when thou hast danced for me, forget not to ask of me whatsoever thou hast a mind to ask. Whatsoever thou shalt desire I will give it thee, even to the half of my kingdom. I have sworn it, have I not?

SALOME. Thou hast sworn it, Tetrarch.

HEROD. And I have never failed of my word. I am not of those who break their oaths. I know not how to lie. I am the slave of my word, and my word is the word of a king. The King of Cappadocia had ever a lying tongue, but he is no true king. He is a coward. Also he owes me money that he will not repay. He has even insulted my ambassadors. He has spoken words that were wounding. But Cæsar will crucify him. And if he crucify him not, yet will he die, being eaten of worms.

The prophet has prophesied it. Well! wherefore dost thou tarry, Salome?

SALOME. I am waiting until my slaves bring perfumes to me and the seven veils, and take from off my feet my sandals.[1]

[*Slaves bring perfumes and the seven veils, and take off the sandals of Salome.*]

HEROD. Ah, thou art to dance with naked feet! 'Tis well! 'Tis well! Thy little feet will be like white doves. They will be like little white flowers that dance upon the trees.... No, no, she is going to dance on blood! There is blood spilt on the ground. She must not dance on blood. It were an evil omen.

HERODIAS. What is it to thee if she dance on blood? Thou hast waded deep enough in it....

HEROD. What is it to me? Ah! look at the moon! She has become red. She has become red as blood. Ah! the prophet prophesied truly. He prophesied that the moon would become as blood. Did he not prophesy it? All of ye heard him prophesying it. And now the moon has become as blood. Do ye not see it?

HERODIAS. Oh yes, I see it well, and the stars are falling like unripe figs, are they not? and the sun is becoming black like sackcloth of hair, and the kings of the earth are afraid. That at least one can see. The prophet is justified of his words in that at least, for truly the kings of the earth are afraid.... Let us go within. You are sick. They will say at Rome that you are mad. Let us go within, I tell you.

THE VOICE OF IOKANAAN. Who is this who cometh from Edom, who is this who cometh from Bozra, whose raiment is dyed with purple, who shineth in the beauty of his garments, who walketh mighty in his greatness?[2] Wherefore is thy raiment stained with scarlet?

---

1 Wilde was the first to identify Salome's performance as "the dance of the seven veils." The trope perhaps calls upon the myth of Ishtar, as related in Appendix A2, pp. 88-89.

2 Isaiah 63:1: "Who is this that cometh from Edom, with dyed garments from Bozrah? This that is glorious in his apparel, travelling in the greatness of his strength? I that speak in righteousness, mighty to save."

HERODIAS. Let us go within. The voice of that man maddens me. I will not have my daughter dance while he is continually crying out. I will not have her dance while you look at her in this fashion. In a word, I will not have her dance.

HEROD. Do not rise, my wife, my queen, it will avail thee nothing. I will not go within till she hath danced. Dance, Salome, dance for me.

HERODIAS. Do not dance, my daughter.

SALOME. I am ready, Tetrarch.

[*Salome dances the dance of the seven veils.*]

HEROD. Ah! wonderful! wonderful! You see that she has danced for me, your daughter. Come near, Salome, come near, that I may give thee thy fee. Ah! I pay a royal price to those who dance for my pleasure. I will pay thee royally. I will give thee whatsoever thy soul desireth. What wouldst thou have? Speak.

SALOME. [*kneeling.*] I would that they presently bring me in a silver charger[1] ...

HEROD. [*laughing.*] In a silver charger? Surely yes, in a silver charger. She is charming, is she not? What is it that thou wouldst have in a silver charger, O sweet and fair Salome, thou that art fairer than all the daughters of Judæa? What wouldst thou have them bring thee in a silver charger? Tell me. Whatsoever it may be, thou shalt receive it. My treasures belong to thee. What is it that thou wouldst have, Salome?

SALOME. [*rising.*] The head of Iokanaan.

HERODIAS. Ah! that is well said, my daughter.

HEROD. No, no!

HERODIAS. That is well said, my daughter.

HEROD. No, no, Salome. It is not that thou desirest. Do not listen to thy mother's voice. She is ever giving thee evil counsel. Do not heed her.

SALOME. It is not my mother's voice that I heed. It is for mine own pleasure that I ask the head of Iokanaan in a silver charger. You have sworn an oath, Herod. Forget not that you have sworn an oath.

---

1 Large, flat, and often decorative platter.

HEROD. I know it. I have sworn an oath by my gods. I know it well. But I pray thee, Salome, ask of me something else. Ask of me the half of my kingdom, and I will give it thee. But ask not of me what thy lips have asked.

SALOME. I ask of you the head of Iokanaan.

HEROD. No, no, I will not give it thee.

SALOME. You have sworn an oath, Herod.

HERODIAS. Yes, you have sworn an oath. Everybody heard you. You swore it before everybody.

HEROD. Peace, woman! It is not to you I speak.

HERODIAS. My daughter has done well to ask the head of Iokanaan. He has covered me with insults. He has said unspeakable things against me. One can see that she loves her mother well. Do not yield, my daughter. He has sworn an oath, he has sworn an oath.

HEROD. Peace! Speak not to me! ... Salome, I pray thee be not stubborn. I have ever been kind toward thee. I have ever loved thee.... It may be that I have loved thee too much. Therefore ask not this thing of me. This is a terrible thing, an awful thing to ask of me. Surely, I think thou art jesting. The head of a man that is cut from his body is ill to look upon, is it not? It is not meet that the eyes of a virgin should look upon such a thing. What pleasure couldst thou have in it. There is no pleasure that thou couldst have in it. No, no, it is not that thou desirest. Hearken to me. I have an emerald, a great emerald and round, that the minion of Cæsar has sent unto me. When thou lookest through this emerald thou canst see that which passeth afar off. Cæsar himself carries such an emerald when he goes to the circus. But my emerald is the larger. I know well that it is the larger. It is the largest emerald in the whole world. Thou wilt take that, wilt thou not? Ask it of me and I will give it thee.

SALOME. I demand the head of Iokanaan.

HEROD. Thou art not listening. Thou art not listening. Suffer me to speak, Salome.

SALOME. The head of Iokanaan.

HEROD. No, no, thou wouldst not have that. Thou sayest that but to trouble me, because that I have looked at thee and ceased not this night. It is true, I have looked at thee and ceased not this night. Thy beauty has troubled me. Thy beauty has grievously troubled me, and I have looked at thee overmuch. Nay, but I will look at thee no more. One should not look at anything. Neither at things, nor at people should one look. Only in mirrors is it well to look, for mirrors do but show us masks. Oh! oh! bring wine! I thirst.... Salome, Salome, let us be as friends. Bethink thee.... Ah! what would I say? What was't? Ah! I remember it! ... Salome,—nay but come nearer to me; I fear thou wilt not hear my words,— Salome, thou knowest my white peacocks, my beautiful white peacocks, that walk in the garden between the myrtles and the tall cypress-trees. Their beaks are gilded with gold and the grains that they eat are smeared with gold, and their feet are stained with purple. When they cry out the rain comes, and the moon shows herself in the heavens when they spread their tails. Two by two they walk between the cypress-trees and the black myrtles, and each has a slave to tend it. Sometimes they fly across the trees, and anon they couch in the grass, and round the pools of the water. There are not in all the world birds so wonderful. I know that Cæsar himself has no birds so fair as my birds. I will give thee fifty of my peacocks. They will follow thee whithersoever thou goest, and in the midst of them thou wilt be like unto the moon in the midst of a great white cloud.... I will give them to thee, all. I have but a hundred, and in the whole world there is no king who has peacocks like unto my peacocks. But I will give them all to thee. Only thou must loose me from my oath, and must not ask of me that which thy lips have asked of me.

[*He empties the cup of wine.*]

SALOME. Give me the head of Iokanaan!

HERODIAS. Well said, my daughter! As for you, you are ridiculous with your peacocks.

HEROD. Peace! you are always crying out. You cry out like a beast of prey. You must not cry in such fashion. Your voice wearies me. Peace, I tell you! ... Salome, think on what thou art doing. It may be that this man comes from God. He is a holy man. The finger of God has touched him. God has put terrible words into his mouth. In the palace, as in the desert, God is ever with him.... It may be that He is, at least. One cannot tell, but it is possible that God is with him and for him. If he die also, peradventure some evil may befall me.

Verily, he has said that evil will befall some one on the day whereon he dies. On whom should it fall if it fall not on me? Remember, I slipped in blood when I came hither. Also did I not hear a beating of wings in the air, a beating of vast wings? These are ill omens. And there were other things. I am sure that there were other things, though I saw them not. Thou wouldst not that some evil should befall me, Salome? Listen to me again.

SALOME. Give me the head of Iokanaan!

HEROD. Ah! thou art not listening to me. Be calm. As for me, am I not calm? I am altogether calm. Listen. I have jewels hidden in this place—jewels that thy mother even has never seen; jewels that are marvelous to look at. I have a collar of pearls, set in four rows. They are like unto moons chained with rays of silver. They are even as half a hundred moons caught in a golden net. On the ivory breast of a queen they have rested. Thou shalt be as fair as a queen when thou wearest them. I have amethysts of two kinds; one that is black like wine, and one that is red like wine that one has coloured with water. I have topazes yellow as are the eyes of tigers, and topazes that are pink as the eyes of a wood-pigeon, and green topazes that are as the eyes of cats. I have opals that burn always, with a flame that is cold as ice, opals that make sad men's minds, and are afraid of the shadows. I have onyxes like the eyeballs of a dead woman. I have moon-stones that change when the moon changes, and are wan when they see the sun. I have sapphires big like eggs, and as blue as blue flowers. The sea wanders within them, and the moon comes never to trouble the blue of their waves. I have chrysolites and beryls, and chrysoprases and rubies; I have sardonyx and hyacinth stones, and stones of chalcedony, and I will give them all unto thee, all, and other things will I add to them. The King of the Indies has but even now sent me four fans fashioned from the feathers of parrots, and the King of Numidia a garment of ostrich feathers. I have a crystal, into which it is not lawful for a woman to look, nor may young men behold it until they have been beaten with rods. In a coffer of nacre I have three wondrous turquoises. He who wears them on his forehead can imagine things which are not, and he who carries them in his hand can turn the fruitful woman into a woman that is barren. These are great treasures. They are treasures above all price. But this is not all. In an ebony coffer I have two cups of amber that are like apples of pure gold. If an enemy pour poison into these cups they becomes like apples of silver. In a coffer incrusted with amber I have sandals incrusted with glass. I have mantles that have been brought from the land of the Seres, and bracelets decked about with carbuncles and with jade that come from the city of Euphrates....[1] What desirest thou more than this, Salome? Tell me the thing that thou desirest, and I will give it thee. All that thou askest I will give thee, save one thing only. I will give thee all that is mine, save only the life of one man. I will give thee the mantle of the high priest. I will give thee the veil of the sanctuary.

THE JEWS. Oh! oh!

SALOME. Give me the head of Iokanaan.

HEROD. [*sinking back in his seat.*] Let her be given what she asks! Of a truth she is her mother's child! [*The first Soldier approaches. Herodias draws from the hand of the Tetrarch the ring of death, and gives it to the Soldier, who straightway bears it to the Executioner. The Executioner looks scared.*] Who has taken my ring? There was a ring on my right hand. Who has drunk my wine? There was wine in my cup. It was full of wine. Some one has drunk it! Oh! surely some evil will befall some one. [*The Executioner goes down into the cistern.*] Ah! Wherefore did I give my oath? Hereafter let no king swear an oath. If he keep it not, it is terrible, and if he keep it, it is terrible also.

---

1   Notably, the precious stones mentioned in this passage also appear in Exodus 39:8-13, where Moses is commanded to create holy vestments with a breastplate described as follows: "And he made the breastplate of cunning work, like the work of the ephod; of gold, blue, and purple, and scarlet, and fine twined linen. / It was foursquare; they made the breastplate double: a span was the length thereof, and a span the breadth thereof, being doubled. / And they set in it four rows of stones: the first row was a sardius, a topaz, and a carbuncle: this was the first row. / And the second row, an emerald, a sapphire, and a diamond. / And the third row, a ligure, an agate, and an amethyst. / And the fourth row, a beryl, an onyx, and a jasper: they were inclosed in ouches of gold in their inclosings." The stones also appear in Ezekiel 28:13: "Thou hast been in Eden the garden of God; every precious stone was thy covering, the sardius, topaz, and the diamond, the beryl, the onyx, and the jasper, the sapphire, the emerald, and the carbuncle, and gold: the workmanship of thy tabrets and of thy pipes was prepared in thee in the day that thou wast created."

HERODIAS. My daughter has done well.

HEROD. I am sure that some misfortune will happen.

SALOME.

[*She leans over the cistern and listens.*]

There is no sound. I hear nothing. Why does he not cry out, this man? Ah! if any man sought to kill me, I would cry out, I would struggle, I would not suffer.... Strike, strike, Naaman, I tell you.... No, I hear nothing. There is a silence, a terrible silence. Ah! something has fallen upon the ground. I heard something fall. It was the sword of the executioner. He is afraid, this slave. He has dropped his sword. He dare not kill him. He is a coward, this slave! Let soldiers be sent. [*She sees the Page of Herodias and addresses him.*] Come hither. Thou wert the friend of him who is dead, wert thou not? Well, I tell thee, there are not dead men enough. Go to the soldiers and bid them go down and bring me the thing I ask, the thing the Tetrarch has promised me, the thing that is mine. [*The Page recoils. She turns to the soldiers.*] Hither, ye soldiers. Get ye down into this cistern and bring me the head of this man. Tetrarch, Tetrarch, command your soldiers that they bring me the head of Iokanaan.

[*A huge black arm, the arm of the Executioner, comes forth from the cistern, bearing on a silver shield the head of Iokanaan. Salome seizes it. Herod hides his face with his cloak. Herodias smiles and fans herself. The Nazarenes fall on their knees and begin to pray.*]

Ah! thou wouldst not suffer me to kiss thy mouth, Iokanaan. Well! I will kiss it now. I will bite it with my teeth as one bites a ripe fruit. Yes, I will kiss thy mouth, Iokanaan. I said it; did I not say it? I said it. Ah! I will kiss it now.... But wherefore dost thou not look at me, Iokanaan? Thine eyes that were so terrible, so full of rage and scorn, are shut now. Wherefore are they shut? Open thine eyes! Lift up thine eyelids, Iokanaan! Wherefore dost thou not look at me? ... And thy tongue, that was like a red snake darting poison, it moves no more, it speaks no words, Iokanaan, that scarlet viper that spat its venom upon me. It is strange, is it not? How is it that the red viper stirs no longer? ... Thou wouldst have none of me, Iokanaan. Thou rejectedst me. Thou didst speak evil words against me. Thou didst bear thyself toward me as to a harlot, as to a woman that is a wanton, to me, Salome, daughter of Herodias, Princess of Judaea! Well, I still live, but thou art dead, and thy head belongs to me. I can do with it what I will. I can throw it to the dogs and to the birds of the air. That which the dogs leave, the birds of the air shall devour....[1] Ah, Iokanaan, Iokanaan, thou wert the man that I loved alone among men! All other men were hateful to me. But thou wert beautiful! Thy body was a column of ivory set upon feet of silver. It was a garden full of doves and lilies of silver. It was a tower of silver decked with shields of ivory. There was nothing in the world so white as thy body. There was nothing in the world so black as thy hair. In the whole world there was nothing so red as thy mouth. Thy voice was a censer[2] that scattered strange perfumes, and when I looked on thee I heard a strange music. Ah! wherefore didst thou not look at me, Iokanaan? With the cloak of thine hands, and with the cloak of thy blasphemies thou didst hide thy face. Thou didst put upon thine eyes the covering of him who would see his God. Well, thou hast seen thy God, Iokanaan, but me, me, thou didst never see. If thou hadst seen me thou hadst loved me. I saw thee, and I loved thee. Oh, how I loved thee! I love thee yet, Iokanaan. I love only thee.... I am athirst for thy beauty; I am hungry for thy body; and neither wine nor apples can appease my desire. What shall I do now, Iokanaan? Neither the floods nor the great waters can quench my passion. I was a princess, and thou didst scorn me. I was a virgin, and thou didst take my virginity from me. I was chaste, and thou didst fill my veins with fire.... Ah! ah! wherefore didst thou not look at me? If thou hadst looked at me thou hadst loved me. Well I know that thou wouldst have loved me, and the mystery of Love is greater than the mystery of Death.[3]

---

1   Deuteronomy 28:25-26: "The LORD shall cause thee to be smitten before thine enemies: thou shalt go out one way against them, and flee seven ways before them: and shalt be removed into all the kingdoms of the earth. / And thy carcase shall be meat unto all fowls of the air, and unto the beasts of the earth, and no man shall fray them away."

2   A vessel designed for burning incense.

3   Conspicuously, Douglas's translation omits the final line of this speech, which was later reintroduced into the script by Robert Ross: "Il ne faut regarder que l'amour," which Ross translates as "Love only should one consider." Literally: "One must look only at love."

HEROD. She is monstrous, thy daughter; I tell thee she is monstrous. In truth, what she has done is a great crime. I am sure that it is a crime against some unknown God.

HERODIAS. I am well pleased with my daughter. She has done well. And I would stay here now.

HEROD. [*rising.*] Ah! There speaks my brother's wife! Come! I will not stay in this place. Come, I tell thee. Surely some terrible thing will befall. Manasseh, Issachar, Ozias, put out the torches.[1] I will not look at things, I will not suffer things to look at me. Put out the torches! Hide the moon! Hide the stars! Let us hide ourselves in our palace, Herodias. I begin to be afraid.

[*The slaves put out the torches. The stars disappear. A great cloud crosses the moon and conceals it completely. The stage becomes quite dark. The Tetrarch begins to climb the staircase.*]

THE VOICE OF SALOME. Ah! I have kissed thy mouth, Iokanaan, I have kissed thy mouth. There was a bitter taste on thy lips. Was it the taste of blood? ... Nay; but perchance it was the taste of love.... They say that love hath a bitter taste.... But what matter? what matter? I have kissed thy mouth, Iokanaan, I have kissed thy mouth.

[*A ray of moonlight falls on Salome and illumines her.*]

HEROD. [*turning round and seeing Salome.*] Kill that woman![2]

[*The soldiers rush forward and crush beneath their shields Salome, daughter of Herodias, Princess of Judaea.*]

CURTAIN

---

1 Manasseh was a king of Judah imprisoned for promoting paganism within his kingdom. According to 2 Chronicles he was restored to the throne after returning his people to the God of Israel. In Genesis, Issachar is the son of Leah and Jacob who founded the Israelite tribe of Issachar. Ozias (also Uzziah) was the king of Judah punished with leprosy for attempting to burn incense in the temple, an office reserved for priests.

2 In Edmond de Goncourt's novel *La Faustin* (1882), the eponymous heroine is an actress who, visiting the deathbed of her lover, resorts to a mere performance of emotion. Seeing through her performance, his dying words are: "Turn out that woman!" Edmond de Goncourt, *La Faustin* (Paris: Bibliothèque Charpentier, 1903), 345.

Appendix A: Sources

1. Matthew 14:1-12, *The Bible: Authorized King James Version with Apocrypha*, ed. Robert Carroll and Stephen Prickett (New York: Oxford UP, 2008)

[Parallel accounts of Salome's story are presented in Mark 6:17-29 and Matthew 14:3-11, though neither text mentions her by name. The details of Salome's birth and familial relations are related in Flavius Josephus's *Jewish Antiquities* (Book XVIII, Chapter 5) without mention of any connection between Salome and the death of John the Baptist.]

1 At that time Herod the tetrarch heard of the fame of Jesus,

2 And said unto his servants, This is John the Baptist; he is risen from the dead; and therefore mighty works do shew forth themselves in him.

3 For Herod had laid hold on John, and bound him, and put *him* in prison for Herodias' sake, his brother Philip's wife.

4 For John said unto him, It is not lawful for thee to have her.

5 And when he would have put him to death, he feared the multitude, because they counted him as a prophet.[1]

6 But when Herod's birthday was kept, the daughter of Herodias danced before them, and pleased Herod.

7 Whereupon he promised with an oath to give her whatsoever she would ask.

8 And she, being before instructed of her mother, said, Give me here John Baptist's head in a charger.

9 And the king was sorry: nevertheless for the oath's sake, and them which sat with him at meat, he commanded *it* to be given *her*.

10 And he sent, and beheaded John in the prison.

11 And his head was brought in a charger, and given to the damsel: and she brought *it* to her mother.

12 And his disciples came, and took up the body, and buried it, and went and told Jesus.

---

1 The Gospel of Mark presents a similar account, though providing a slightly different rationale for Herod's unwillingness to execute John the Baptist: "For Herod feared John, knowing that he was a just man and an holy, and observed him; and when he heard him, he did many things, and heard him gladly" (Mark 6:20).

2. "Descent of the Goddess Ishtar into the Lower World," *The Sacred Books and Early Literature of the East*, ed. Charles Francis Home, 235-41 (New York: Parke, Austin, and Lipscomb, 1917), 237-38

[Although Wilde's text conspicuously omits any description of Salome's dance, it has traditionally been treated as a climactic moment in performances of the play. The "dance of the seven veils" may well originate in the myth of Ishtar (Isis), the Assyrian and Babylonian goddess of fertility, sexuality, eros, and war. According to this account, Ishtar's descent into the underworld results in the cessation of all sexual activity in the secular world. The gatekeeper requires that she shed one article of clothing after passing through each of the seven gates that enclose the underworld.[1]]

He bade her enter the first gate, which he opened wide, and took the large crown off her head:
"Why, O gatekeeper, dost thou remove the large crown off my head?"
"Enter, O lady, such are the decrees of Ereshkigal."
The second gate he bade her enter, opening it wide, and removed her earrings:
"Why, O gatekeeper, dost thou remove my earrings?"
"Enter, O lady, for such are the decrees of Ereshkigal."
The third gate he bade her enter, opened it wide, and removed her necklace:
"Why, O gatekeeper, dost thou remove my necklace?"
"Enter, O lady, for such are the decrees of Ereshkigal."
The fourth gate he bade her enter, opened it wide, and removed the ornaments of her breast:
"Why, O gatekeeper, dost thou remove the ornaments of my breast?"
"Enter, O lady, for such are the decrees of Ereshkigal."
The fifth gate he bade her enter, opened it wide, and removed the girdle of her body studded with birthstones.

---

1 According to Jess Sully, Constance Wilde is rumored to have belonged to the Hermetic Order of the Golden Dawn, in which Ishtar plays an important role: "The society was composed of ten grades, each successive order veiled from the previous one by the veils of Isis and Isis's sister Nephthys. When Isis unveiled and revealed her secret, mankind would learn the truth of the world's most ancient, and therefore most divine, religion. To know the secret was to come face to face with the true God" (25). Jess Sully, "Narcissistic Princess, Rejected Lover, Veiled Priestess, Virtuous Virgin: How Oscar Wilde Imagined Salomé," *Wildean: A Journal of Oscar Wilde Studies* 25 (July 2004): 16-33.

"Why, O gatekeeper, dost thou remove the girdle of my body, studded with birth-stones?"

"Enter, O lady, for such are the decrees of Ereshkigal."

The sixth gate, he bade her enter, opened it wide, and removed the spangles off her hands and feet.

"Why, O gatekeeper, dost thou remove the spangles off my hands and feet?"

"Enter, O lady, for such are the decrees of Ereshkigal."

The seventh gate he bade her enter, opened it wide, and removed her loin-cloth.

"Why, O gatekeeper, dost thou remove my loin-cloth?"

"Enter, O lady, for such are the decrees of Ereshkigal."

Now when Ishtar had gone down into the land of no return,
Ereshkigal saw her and was angered at her presence.
Ishtar, without reflection, threw herself at her [in a rage].
Ereshkigal opened her mouth and spoke,
To Namtar,[1] her messenger, she addressed herself:
"Go Namtar, imprison her in my palace.
Send against her sixty disease, to punish Ishtar.
Eye-disease against her eyes,
Disease of the side against her side,
Foot-disease against her foot,
Heart-disease against her heart,
Head-disease against her head,
Against her whole being, against her entire body."
After the lady Ishtar had gone down into the land of no return,
The bull did not mount the cow, the ass approached not the she-ass,
To the maid in the street, no man drew near
The man slept in his apartment,
The maid slept by herself.

3. From Heinrich Heine, *Atta Troll*, trans. Herman Scheffauer (New York: B.W. Huebsch, [1843] 1914), 113-15

[Heine's mock epic *Atta Troll* (1843) tells the story of a dancing bear who escapes from captivity and becomes the leader of a plot to overthrow his human captors. On Saint John's Eve, Atta Troll witnesses the passing of The Wild Hunt, a procession of mythic demons and notorious villains. Herodias is among the party. Strikingly, Heine speculates on the possibility that Herodias may not have despised John the

---

1   A minor deity and the son of Ereshkigal, who is reputedly responsible for pestilence in the secular world.

Baptist at all. Here, as in Wilde's *Salome*, violence is conspicuously conflated with sensuality and desire.]

Whether devil this or saint
Know I not. With women, ah,
None can ever know where saint
Ends nor where the fiend begins.

All the magic of the East
Lay within her glowing face,
And her dress brought memories
Of Scheherazadê's[1] tales.

Lips as red as pomegranates
And a curved nose lily white,
Limbs as slender and as cool
As some green oasis-palm.

From her palfrey[2] white she leaned,
Flanked by giant Moors who trod
Close beside the queenly dame
Holding up the golden reins.

Of most royal blood was she,
She the Queen of old Judea,
She great Herod's lovely wife,
She who craved the Baptist's head.

For this crimson crime was she
Banned and cursed. Now in this chase
Must she ride, a wandering spook,
Till the dawn of Judgment Day.

---

1 The Persian queen, wife of Shahryar, and storyteller of *One Thousand and One Nights*. Prior to their marriage, Shahryar marries a new bride every day only to have her executed the following morning. Scheherazade breaks this cycle through the power of storytelling. Each night, Scheherazade tells Shahryar a story but delays concluding her tale until the next day. The king is thus compelled to spare her life from one day to the next. By the time Scheherazade has exhausted her store of stories, Shahryar has fallen in love with her.

2 A horse characterized by an easy gait.

Still within her hands she bears
That deep charger with the head
Of the Prophet, still she kisses—
Kisses it with fiery lips.

For she loved the Prophet once,
Though the Bible naught reveals,
Yet her blood-stained love lives on
Storied in her people's hearts.

How might else a man declare
All the longing of this lady?
Would a woman crave the head
Of a man she did not love?

She perchance was slightly vexed
With her darling, and was moved
To behead him, but when she
On the trencher saw his head,

Then she wept and lost her wits
Dying in love's madness straight.
(What! Love's madness? Pleonasm!
Love itself is madness still!)

Rising nightly from her grave,
To this frenzied hunt she hies,
In her hands the gory head
Which with feline joy she flings

High into the air betimes,
Laughing like a wanton child,
Cleverly she catches it
Like some idle rubber ball.

4. From J.C. Heywood, *Herodias: A Dramatic Poem* (New York: Hurd and Houghton, 1867), 210-15

[Heywood wrote three dramatic poems touching on the story of Salome: *Salome* (1862), *Herodias* (1867), and *Antonius* (1867). The following passage is noteworthy for its depiction of Herodias apostrophizing and ultimately kissing the decapitated head of John the Baptist. Wilde innovates on this scene in his own account by presenting Salome, rather than Herodias, as the prophet's sinister admirer.]

Herodias with John Baptist's Head.

Herodias.

At length I am avenged; drink, drink, my soul,
The sweet conviction, drink till thou be drunk.
The king, smitten of God, before his time,
Eaten, alive, of worms, in torment howls,
Calleth for death that comes not, shall not come,
Till all the horrors of the sepulcher,
The crawling, gnawing worms, slow-feeding fires
Which open their dull phosphorescent eyes
Only in darkness, putrefaction black,
And stifling mould, which shoots its creeping roots
And grows to forests, crushing flesh to dust,
Shall in his life be felt; his body thus,
Not dying but consumed, his soul shall go
Swift to black Hades[1] and Tartarian[2] woe.
Salome, from the world self-banished,
Seeketh to find her exile in the world,
And by self-punishment to make amends;
Self-judging, self-accused, and ignorant
That man may pray and pray and still be damned,
May practice charity and still be damned,
Inflict self-punishment and still be damned;
Forgetful that, if there be real offence,
Th'offended power alone can name the price
Of full forgiveness—'tis her fantasy,
Led on by virtue—virtue's such a fool!
And thou, sweet head, yes, thou art mind at last.

What! Thou canst smile while I do speak to thee!
I thought my voice, like a storm-breeding wind,
Would drive that smile away, and bring a frown
To flash its lightnings from the brow of heaven.

---

1 Refers both to the ancient Greek god of the underworld and to the abode of the dead.
2 Refers to Tartarus, in Greek mythology a site devoted to punishment of the wicked.

Thy heart's too stony that I will not have.
I wonder it could give even these red drop.—
Come they indeed from thee? I'll taste this blood.
Methinks I'd know the taste of thine own blood.
I would have mingled all thy blood with mine,
And sent it forth in such heaven-daring life
That e'en Prometheus[1] in comparison
Should fail in enterprise, and all the Titans[2]
Pigmies and cowards be; could that not be,
I would have given all my blood to thee.
But thou disdainedst me; from these smiling lips
I've heard the only words I ever heard
Since tearful Innocence bid me good-bye,
A weary time ago, could make my blood
Mount from my heart to watch-towers of my cheeks,
To see who thus so loudly summoned it.
Thou'st paid the penalty of thy disdain.
Where was thy God? Could He not save thee, then?
Is there then naught a woman may not do?
Now will I e'en defy thy God Himself,
And in His temple will I make my bed,
And on His altar will dream dreams of thee,
My sweet: some living semblance of thyself,
With blood that floweth not so cold as thine,
To be my fellow in the holiest place.
What! thou dost frown at last! 'tis thine old trick,
When I did meet thee. 'Twill not fright me now,
Nor turn me back, nor make me hold my tongue.
Now thou art mine, I can embrace thee even,
And weave my lily fingers in thy hair,
And stroke thy temples, fondle thee, and hate.
Call thyself back to life, and list to me
While here I mock thee, spurn thee, spit on thee.[3]
Why liest thou there? What! would'st thou plead to me?
Ah! Thou art very pale; where is the health
That blossomed like a garden in thy face,

---

1 In Greek mythology, the Titan who forged man out of clay and, by some
   accounts, stole fire from Zeus and gave it to humanity.
2 In Greek mythology, the first pantheon of gods and goddesses, eventually to
   be overthrown by the Olympians.
3 This passage anticipates Wilde's depiction of Salome, who demands that the
   page of Herodias bring to her "the thing that is mine" and subsequently
   caresses the severed head of Iokanaan (p. 83).

And brought forth manly beauty? where the flush
Of indignation or of shame whene'er
I spoke to thee? Come, let me call it back
With words would shame the satyrs in their dens.
It comes not! what! comes not! Thy virtue sleeps,
And all thy blushes which have guarded it
Have run away to cool in this flat dish.
I'll with my fingers put them in their place
On thy pale cheeks, yea, even on thy brow,
Or summon them with my all-potent kiss.
Come, let me press thy virtuous, scornful lips—

5. From Oscar Wilde, "Review of J.C. Heywood's *Salome*" [excerpted from "The Poet's Corner"], *Pall Mall Gazette* (15 February 1888): 291-92

Mr. Heywood's *Salome* seems to have thrilled the critics of the United States. From a collection of press notices prefixed to the volume we learn that *Putnam's Magazine* has found in it "the simplicity and grace of naked Grecian statues," and that Dr. Jos. G. Cogswell, LL.D.,[1] has declared that it will live to be appreciated "as long as the English language endures." Remembering that prophecy is the most gratuitous form of error, we will not attempt to argue with Dr. Jos. G. Cogswell, LL.D., but will content ourselves with protesting against such a detestable expression as "naked Grecian statues." If this be the literary style of the future the English language will not endure very long. As for the poem itself, the best that one can say of it is that it is a triumph of conscientious industry. From an artistic point of view it is a very commonplace production indeed, and we must protest against such blank verse as the following:

From the hour I saw her first, I was entranced,
Or embosomed in a charmed world, circumscribed
By its proper circumambient atmosphere,
Herself its centre, and wide pervading spirit.
The air all beauty of colour held dissolved,
And tints distilled as dew are shed by heaven.

---

1 Librarian, educator, and reviewer who contributed to *Blackwood's Edinburgh Magazine*, *The New York Review*, and other major organs of nineteenth-century criticism.

6. From Stéphane Mallarmé, "La scène: Nourrice—Hérodiade," *The Poems in Verse*, trans. Peter Manson, 59-89 (Oxford, OH: Miami UP, [1864-67] 2012), 69-71, 79-81

[Mallarmé's poem provides the reader with a glimpse into Herodias's life prior to her marriage to Herod. In the scene excerpted here, a young Herodias addresses her nurse, conflating chastity and desire in a way that anticipates Wilde's rendering of Salome.]

Get back.
The blond torrent of my spotless hair
when it bathes my solitary body freezes it
with horror, and each hair, wound up in light
is immortal. O woman, a kiss would kill me
if beauty were not death.
    By what lure
drawn and what morning forgotten by the prophets
pours its sad feasts on the dying distances—
do I know? You have seen me, winter nurse,
enter the heavy prison of stones and iron
where the wildcat centuries of my old lions drag
and I walked, fated, my hands unharmed,
in the desert perfume of those former kings:
but have you already seen what my fears were?
I halt, dreaming of exiles, and unpetal,
as if by a pool whose fountain welcomes me,
the pale lilies that are in me, while, following
with love-struck eyes the languid fragments
falling in silence through my reverie,
the lions, sweeping aside my lazy robe,
look at my feet that would becalm the sea.
Calm the shivering of your senile flesh:
come while my hair adopts the too savage
style that reminds you of your fear of manes,
and help me, since you dare not see me so,
to comb it nonchalantly in a mirror.

[...]

Yes, it's for me—for me—that I flower, deserted!
You know it, amethyst gardens, buried
endlessly in dazzled, learned gulfs,
unknown golds, hiding your antique light

under the somber sleep of a primal earth,
you, stones from which my eyes' pure jewels
borrow melodious brilliance, and you
metals that give to my young hair
a fatal splendor and its massive impetus!
As for you, woman born in malignant centuries
for the spite of sibylline caves,
who speak of a mortal! according to whom, from the chalices[1]
· of my robes, aroma of fierce delights,
the white shiver of my nudity would exit,
prophecy that if the summer's lukewarm blue
towards which woman natively undresses,
sees me in my trembling starlike modesty, I will die!

I love the horror of being virgin and I want
to live inside the fear my hair causes me
so that, at evening, withdrawn on my couch, inviolate
reptile, I might feel in my useless flesh
the cold scintillation of your pale brilliance,
you on the point of death, you who burn with chastity,
white night of icicles and cruel snow!

7. From Gustave Flaubert, "Hérodias," *The Complete Works of Gustave Flaubert*, Vol. 4, 1-52 (New York: M. Walter Dunne, [1877] 1904), 45-48

[While still at Oxford, Walter Pater loaned Wilde a copy of "Hérodias" (1877), a text that apparently made quite an impression on the young writer. According to William Rothenstein, Wilde acknowledged the enormous influence of this work upon *Salome*, while also noting that the two texts differ widely in their treatment of the narrative. "In literature," Wilde quipped, "it is always necessary to kill one's father."[2] As in Wilde's account, Flaubert presents Iaokanann as an enigmatic prophet who denounces Herodias as a wanton adulteress and frequently reverts to the use of simile. Especially noteworthy is Flaubert's

---

1 Usually, a chalice denotes a ceremonial cup, especially one used in Catholic rituals to hold the wine of the Eucharist. The term also describes the cup-shaped interior of a blossom. In this passage, it describes the physical layers of Herodias's robes, thus continuing the passage's appeal to sensual imagery.

2 William Rothenstein, *Men and Memories: Recollections of William Rothenstein, 1872-1900* (London: Faber and Faber, 1932), 184. Appropriately, the quip was originally uttered in French: "Dans la littérature il faut toujours tuer son père."

depiction of Salome's dance before the throne of Herod. Although Flaubert's Salome serves chiefly as the mouthpiece of Herodias, departing from the room momentarily to learn her mother's bidding, her presence—at once sensual and numinous—reflects the almost mystic power she would wield in Wilde's account.]

Through a drapery of filmy blue gauze that veiled her head and throat, her arched eyebrows, tiny ears, and ivory-white skin could be distinguished. A scarf of shot-silk fell from her shoulders, and was caught up at the waist by a girdle of fretted silver. Her full trousers, of black silk, were embroidered in a pattern of silver mandragoras,[1] and as she moved forward with indolent grace, her little feet were seen to be shod with slippers made of the feathers of humming-birds.

When she arrived in front of the pavilion she removed her veil. Behold! she seemed to be Herodias herself, as she had appeared in the days of her blooming youth.

Immediately the damsel began to dance before the tetrarch. Her slender feet took dainty steps to the rhythm of a flute and a pair of Indian bells. Her round white arms seemed ever beckoning and striving to entice to her side some youth who was fleeing from her allurements. She appeared to pursue him, with movements light as a butterfly; her whole mien was like that of an inquisitive Psyche,[2] or a floating spirit that might at any moment dissolve and disappear.

Presently the plaintive notes of the gingras, a small flute of Phoenician origin, replaced the tinkling bells. The attitudes of the dancing nymph now denoted overpowering lassitude. Her bosom heaved with sighs, and her whole being expressed profound languor, although it was not clear whether she sighed for an absent swain or was expiring of love in his embrace. With half-closed eyes and quivering form, she

---

1 Mandrakes, a plant whose roots sometimes assume the shape of human bodies and have been used in pagan rituals.

2 In Greek mythology, a beautiful princess who becomes the lover of Eros, son of Aphrodite. Aphrodite agrees to permit the marriage of Psyche and Eros only if she can live with her husband without ever seeing his face. Fearful that her husband might be a monster, Psyche lights a candle to view his face and is astonished to find that she has married Eros, the very embodiment of beauty. Hurt by her lack of trust, Eros flees. Psyche seeks assistance from Aphrodite, who agrees to reunite the couple only if Psyche accomplishes four arduous tasks. The final task is to obtain a portion of beauty from Persephone, queen of the underworld, and to bring it to Aphrodite in a box. Once again unable to resist her curiosity, Psyche opens the box and finds, instead of beauty, sleep. When Eros discovers Psyche asleep, he asks Zeus to awaken her and to make her an immortal.

caused mysterious undulations to flow downward over her whole body, like rippling waves, while her face remained impassive and her twinkling feet still moved in their intricate steps.

[...]

And now the graceful dancer appeared transported with the very delirium of love and passion. She danced like the priestesses of India, like the Nubians of the cataracts,[1] or like the Bacchantes of Lydia.[2] She whirled about like a flower blown by the tempest. The jewels in her ears sparkled, her swift movements made the colors of her draperies appear to run into one another. Her arms, her feet, her clothing even, seemed to emit streams of magnetism, that set the spectators' blood on fire.

Suddenly the thrilling chords of a harp rang through the hall, and the throng burst into loud acclamations. All eyes were fixed upon Salome, who paused in her rhythmic dance, placed her feet wider apart, and without bending the knees, suddenly swayed her lithe body downward, so that her chin touched the floor; and her whole audience,—nomads, accustomed to a life of privation and abstinence, and the Roman soldiers, expert in debaucheries, the avaricious publicans, and even the crabbed, elderly priests—gazed upon her with dilated nostrils.

Next she began to whirl frantically around the table where Antipas the tetrarch was seated. He leaned towards the flying figure, and in a voice half choked with the voluptuous sighs of a made desire, he sighed: "Come to me! Come!" But she whirled on, while the music of dulcimers swelled louder and the excited spectators roared their applause.

The tetrarch called again, louder than before: "Come to me! Come! Thou shalt have Capernaum,[3] the plains of Tiberias![4] my citadels! yea, the half of my kingdom!"

Again the dancer paused; then, like a flash, she threw herself upon the palms of her hands, while her feet rose straight up into the air. In

---

1 The Cataracts marked the boundary of Nubia, a region located along the Nile River.

2 A priestess of Bacchus (Roman god of wine) and one of the gods recognized in the ancient Roman Province of Lydia.

3 Ancient fishing town, reported in Matthew 4:13 to have been the home of Christ.

4 City on the Sea of Galilee long regarded as one of the four holy cities of Judaism. The Jerusalem Talmud was produced in Tiberius, which served as a thriving center for Jewish intellectual life in the eighteenth and nineteenth centuries.

this bizarre pose she moved about upon the floor like a gigantic beetle; then stood motionless.

The nape of her neck formed a right angle with her vertebrae. The full silken skirts of pale hues that enveloped her limbs when she stood erect, now fell to her shoulders and surrounded her face like a rainbow. Her lips were tinted a deep crimson, her arched eyebrows were black as jet, her glowing eyes had an almost terrible radiance; and the tiny drops of perspiration on her forehead looked like dew upon white marble.

She made no sound; and the burning gaze of that multitude of men was concentrated upon her.

A sound like the snapping of fingers came from the gallery over the pavilion. Instantly, with one of her movements of bird-like swiftness, Salome stood erect. The next moment she rapidly passed up a flight of steps leading to the gallery, and coming to the front of it she leaned over, smiled upon the tetrarch and with an air of almost childlike naïveté, pronounced these words:

"I ask my lord to give me, placed upon a charger, the head of—" She hesitated, as if not certain of the name; then said: "The head of Iaokanann!"

8. William Wilde, "Salome," *Dublin Verses by Members of Trinity College* (London: E. Matthews, [1878] 1895), 150

[Wilde's brother William ("Willie") Wilde wrote a poem on the subject of Salome, originally printed in 1878 in *Kottabos*, a magazine published annually at Trinity College. The poem is noteworthy chiefly for the suggestion, conveyed in the final two lines, that Salome may regard John the Baptist as an object of both loathing and desire.]

The sight of me was a devouring flame
Burning their hearts with fire so wantonly
That night I danced for all his men to see!
Fearless and reckless; for all maiden shame
Strange passion-poisons throbbing overcame
As every eye was riveted on me,
And every soul was mine, mine utterly,—
And thrice each throat cried out aloud my name!

"Ask what thou wilt," black-bearded Herod said.
God wot a weird thing do I crave for prize:
"Give me, I pray thee, presently the head
Of John the Baptist." 'Twixt my hands it lies.
"Ah mother! see! the lips, the half-closed eyes—
Dost think he hates us still, now he is dead?"

9. From Joris-Karl Huysmans, *À Rebours* (New York: Albert and Charles Boni, [1884] 1922), 90-99

[Huysmans's novel *À Rebours* (1884) chronicles the tastes, experiences, and reflections of Jean Des Esseintes, an eccentric aristocrat and aesthete. Wilde was a great admirer of the novel and admitted that Huysmans's description of Gustave Moreau's paintings was a direct influence on his own work.]

For the delight of his spirit and the joy of his eyes, he had desired a few suggestive creations that cast him into an unknown world, revealing to him the contours of new conjectures, agitating the nervous system by the violent deliriums, complicated nightmares, nonchalant or atrocious chimeræ they induced.

Among these were some executed by an artist whose genius allured and entranced him: Gustave Moreau.[1]

Des Esseintes had acquired his two masterpieces and, at night, used to sink into revery before one of them—a representation of Salomé, conceived in this fashion:

A throne, resembling the high altar of a cathedral, reared itself beneath innumerable vaults leaping from heavy Romanesque pillars, studded with polychromatic bricks, set with mosaics, incrusted with lapis lazuli and sardonyx, in a palace that, like a basilica, was at once Mohammedan and Byzantine in design.

In the center of the tabernacle, surmounting an altar approached by semi-circular steps, sat Herod the Tetrarch, a tiara upon his head, his legs pressed closely together, his hands resting upon his knees.

His face was the color of yellow parchment; it was furrowed with wrinkles, ravaged with age. His long beard floated like a white cloud upon the star-like clusters of jewels constellating the orphrey[2] robe fitting tightly over his breast.

Around this form, frozen into the immobile, sacerdotal, hieratic pose of a Hindoo god, burned perfumes wafting aloft clouds of incense which were perforated, like phosphorescent eyes of beasts, by the fiery rays of the stones set in the throne. Then the vapor rolled up, diffusing itself beneath arcades where the blue smoke mingled with the gold powder of the long sunbeams falling from the domes.

In the perverse odor of the perfumes, in the overheated atmosphere of the temple, Salomé, her left arm outstretched in a gesture of command, her right arm drawn back and holding a large lotus on a

---

1 See Appendix B1, p. 108.
2 An elaborate embroidery, often adorning clerical vestments.

level with her face, slowly advances on her toes, to the rhythm of a stringed instrument played by a woman seated on the ground.

Her face is meditative, solemn, almost august, as she commences the lascivious dance that will awaken the slumbering senses of old Herod. Diamonds scintillate against her glistening skin. Her bracelets, her girdles, her rings flash. On her triumphal robe, seamed with pearls, flowered with silver and laminated with gold, the breastplate of jewels, each link of which is a precious stone, flashes serpents of fire against the pallid flesh, delicate as a tea-rose: its jewels like splendid insects with dazzling elytra,[1] veined with carmine, dotted with yellow gold, diapered with blue steel, speckled with peacock green.

With a tense concentration, with the fixed gaze of a somnambulist, she beholds neither the trembling Tetrarch, nor her mother, the fierce Herodias who watches her, nor the hermaphrodite, nor the eunuch who sits, sword in hand, at the foot of the throne—a terrible figure, veiled to his eyes, whose breasts droop like gourds under his orange-checkered tunic.

This conception of Salomé, so haunting to artists and poets, had obsessed Des Esseintes for years. How often had he read in the old Bible of Pierre Variquet, translated by the theological doctors of the University of Louvain, the Gospel of Saint Matthew who, in brief and ingenuous phrases, recounts the beheading of the Baptist![2] How often had he fallen into revery, as he read these lines:

But when Herod's birthday was kept, the daughter of Herodias danced before them, and pleased Herod.

Whereupon he promised with an oath to give her whatsoever she would ask.

And she, being before instructed of her mother, said: Give me here John Baptist's head in a charger.

And the king was sorry: nevertheless, for the oath's sake, and them which sat with him at meat, he commanded it to be given her.

And he sent, and beheaded John in the prison.

And his head was brought in a charger, and given to the damsel: and she brought it to her mother.

But neither Saint Matthew, nor Saint Mark, nor Saint Luke, nor the other Evangelists had emphasized the maddening charms and depravities of the dancer. She remained vague and hidden, mysterious and swooning in the far-off mist of the centuries, not to be grasped by vulgar and materialistic minds, accessible only to disordered and vol-

---

1 The forewings of a beetle.

2 The ornate and antiquated edition to which Des Esseintes refers was published in 1683.

canic intellects made visionaries by their neuroticism; rebellious to painters of the flesh, to Rubens who disguised her as a butcher's wife of Flanders; a mystery to all the writers who had never succeeded in portraying the disquieting exaltation of this dancer, the refined grandeur of this murderess.[1]

In Gustave Moreau's work, conceived independently of the Testament themes, Des Esseintes at last saw realized the superhuman and exotic Salomé of his dreams. She was no longer the mere performer who wrests a cry of desire and of passion from an old man by a perverted twisting of her loins; who destroys the energy and breaks the will of a king by trembling breasts and quivering belly. She became, in a sense, the symbolic deity of indestructible lust, the goddess of immortal Hysteria, of accursed Beauty, distinguished from all others by the catalepsy which stiffens her flesh and hardens her muscles; the monstrous Beast, indifferent, irresponsible, insensible, baneful, like the Helen[2] of antiquity, fatal to all who approach her, all who behold her, all whom she touches.

Thus understood, she was associated with the theogonies[3] of the Far East. She no longer sprang from biblical traditions, could no longer even be assimilated with the living image of Babylon, the royal Prostitute of the Apocalypse,[4] garbed like her in jewels and purple, and painted like her; for she was not hurled by a fatidical[5] power, by a supreme force, into the alluring vileness of debauchery.

The painter, moreover, seems to have wished to affirm his desire of remaining outside the centuries, scorning to designate the origin, nation and epoch, by placing his Salomé in this extraordinary palace with its confused and imposing style, in clothing her with sumptuous

---

1 Peter Paul Rubens (1577-1640) produced two paintings of Salome: "Salome Receives the Head of John the Baptist" and "Herod's Feast," both of which update the story by adorning human figures in seventeenth-century costume.

2 In Greek mythology, the daughter of Zeus, whose abduction by Paris leads to war between Troy and Sparta.

3 A theogony recounts the origins and genesis of divine beings.

4 In Revelations, the Whore of Babylon is associated with the coming of the Antichrist: "And the woman was arrayed in purple and scarlet colour, and decked with gold and precious stones and pearls, having a golden cup in her hand full of abominations and filthiness of her fornication: / And upon her forehead was a name written, MYSTERY, BABYLON THE GREAT, THE MOTHER OF HARLOTS AND ABOMINATIONS OF THE EARTH. / And I saw the woman drunken with the blood of the saints, and with the blood of the martyrs of Jesus: and when I saw her, I wondered with great admiration" (Revelations 17:4-6).

5 Prophetic.

and chimerical robes, in crowning her with a fantastic mitre[1] shaped like a Phœnician tower, such as Salammbô[2] bore, and placing in her hand the sceptre of Isis,[3] the tall lotus, sacred flower of Egypt and India.

Des Esseintes sought the sense of this emblem. Had it that phallic significance which the primitive cults of India gave it? Did it enunciate an oblation of virginity to the senile Herod, an exchange of blood, an impure and voluntary wound, offered under the express stipulation of a monstrous sin? Or did it represent the allegory of fecundity, the Hindoo myth of life, an existence held between the hands of woman, distorted and trampled by the palpitant hands of man whom a fit of madness seizes, seduced by a convulsion of the flesh?[4]

Perhaps, too, in arming his enigmatic goddess with the venerated lotus, the painter had dreamed of the dancer, the mortal woman with the polluted Vase,[5] from whom spring all sins and crimes. Perhaps he had recalled the rites of ancient Egypt, the sepulchral ceremonies of the embalming when, after stretching the corpse on a bench of jasper, extracting the brain with curved needles through the chambers of the nose, the chemists and the priests, before gilding the nails and teeth and coating the body with bitumens[6] and essences, inserted the chaste

---

1   Ceremonial headgear or crown.

2   The eponymous heroine of Gustave Flaubert's 1862 novel about the daughter of a Carthaginian general who must retrieve the stolen veil of the goddess Tanit from a mercenary, Matho, who is also her lover. When he is tortured and executed for his crimes, Salammbô dies of grief. The narrator describes her hair as being ornately piled upon her head, much like a tower: "Her hair was powdered with violet dust, and, according to the fashion of Canaanite maidens, it was gathered up in the form of a tower on the crown of her head, making her appear taller." Flaubert, *Salammbô* (London: Saxon and Co., 1886), 14.

3   Ancient Egyptian goddess of nature, magic, and children. She is often represented as holding a lotus, an Egyptian symbol of creation and rebirth.

4   Likely a reference to the story of Shiva and Parvati. Parvati is said to have created a child, Ganesha, entirely on her own. Most accounts indicate that Parvati's husband, Shiva, tore the head from Ganesha's body during a conflict. Later, Shiva restored Ganesha to life, replacing his head with that of an elephant.

5   Likely a reference to Pandora, in Greek mythology the first woman created by the gods. In some accounts, Pandora is described as a dancer who learns her art from the Muses. Famously, Pandora's curiosity leads her to peer into a container given to her by the gods. By opening the box, Pandora releases evil into the world. Although colloquially referred to as "Pandora's box," the original Greek word for the container was "pithos," a large vase used to store wine, food, and in some cases human remains.

6   Pigments.

petals of the divine flower in the sexual parts, to purify them.

However this may be, an irresistible fascination emanated from this painting; but the water-color entitled *The Apparition* was perhaps even more disturbing.

There, the palace of Herod arose like an Alhambra[1] on slender, iridescent columns with moorish tile, joined with silver béton[2] and gold cement. Arabesques proceeded from lozenges of lapis lazuli, wove their patterns on the cupolas where, on nacreous marquetry, crept rainbow gleams and prismatic flames.

The murder was accomplished. The executioner stood impassive, his hands on the hilt of his long, blood-stained sword.

The severed head of the saint stared lividly on the charger resting on the slabs; the mouth was discolored and open, the neck crimson, and tears fell from the eyes. The face was encircled by an aureole worked in mosaic, which shot rays of light under the porticos and illuminated the horrible ascension of the head, brightening the glassy orbs of the contracted eyes which were fixed with a ghastly stare upon the dancer.

With a gesture of terror, Salomé thrusts from her the horrible vision which transfixes her, motionless, to the ground. Her eyes dilate, her hands clasp her neck in a convulsive clutch.

She is almost nude. In the ardor of the dance, her veils had become loosened. She is garbed only in gold-wrought stuffs and limpid stones; a neck-piece clasps her as a corselet does the body and, like a superb buckle, a marvelous jewel sparkles on the hollow between her breasts. A girdle encircles her hips, concealing the upper part of her thighs, against which beats a gigantic pendant streaming with carbuncles and emeralds.

All the facets of the jewels kindle under the ardent shafts of light escaping from the head of the Baptist. The stones grow warm, outlining the woman's body with incandescent rays, striking her neck, feet and arms with tongues of fire,—vermilions like coals, violets like jets of gas, blues like flames of alcohol, and whites like star light.

The horrible head blazes, bleeding constantly, clots of sombre purple on the ends of the beard and hair. Visible for Salomé alone, it does not, with its fixed gaze, attract Herodias, musing on her finally consummated revenge, nor the Tetrarch who, bent slightly forward, his hands on his knees, still pants, maddened by the nudity of the woman

---

1 A Moorish palace and fortress in Granada, Spain, constructed in 889 CE. It is known for its high, ornamental ceilings and was designed to reflect the beauty and luxury of heaven on earth.

2 Concrete (French).

saturated with animal odors, steeped in balms, exuding incense and myrrh.

Like the old king, Des Esseintes remained dumbfounded, overwhelmed and seized with giddiness, in the presence of this dancer who was less majestic, less haughty but more disquieting than the Salomé of the oil painting.

In this insensate and pitiless image, in this innocent and dangerous idol, the eroticism and terror of mankind were depicted. The tall lotus had disappeared, the goddess had vanished; a frightful nightmare now stifled the woman, dizzied by the whirlwind of the dance, hypnotized and petrified by terror.

It was here that she was indeed Woman, for here she gave rein to her ardent and cruel temperament. She was living, more refined and savage, more execrable and exquisite. She more energetically awakened the dulled senses of man, more surely bewitched and subdued his power of will, with the charm of a tall venereal flower, cultivated in sacrilegious beds, in impious hothouses.

10. From Maurice Maeterlinck, *La Princesse Maleine*, trans. Richard Hovey (New York: Dodd, Mead, [1889] 1911), 17-18

[Wilde was asked to compose the introduction for an edition of Maeterlinck's *La Princesse Maleine* in 1891. Though he did not accept the commission, he appreciated Maeterlinck's work and cited him as an influence when discussing his own decision to compose *Salome* in French: "A great deal of the curious effect that Maeterlinck produces comes from the fact that he, a Flamand by race, writes in an alien language" (Appendix E6, p. 137). The influence of this work is especially apparent in the use of terse repetition throughout the opening scene.]

Act First

Scene 1.—*The gardens of the castle.*
Enter STEPHANO *and* VANOX

VANOX.
What time is it?

STEPHANO.
It must be midnight, judging by the moon.

VANOX.
I think it will rain.

STEPHANO.

Yes; there are great clouds in the west. We shall not be relieved until the fete is ended.

VANOX.

That will not be before daybreak.

STEPHANO.

Oh! oh! Vanox!

[*Here a comet appears over the castle.*]

VANOX.

What?

STEPHANO.

Again the comet of the other night!

VANOX.

It is enormous.

STEPHANO.

It looks as though it dripped blood on the castle.

[*Here a shower of stars seems to fall upon the castle.*]

VANOX.

The stars are falling on the castle! Look! look! look!

STEPHANO.

I never saw such a shower of stars! You would say Heaven wept over this betrothal.

VANOX.

They say all this presages great disasters.

STEPHANO.

Yes,—wars, perhaps, or the death of kings. Such omens were observed when the old king Marcellus died.

VANOX.

They say those stars with long girl's-hair announce the death of princesses.

STEPHANO.

They say ... they say many things.

Appendix B: A Visual History

1. Gustave Moreau, "The Apparition" (1876)

[According to Gomez Carillo, "For Wilde only the painting of Gustave Moreau (1826-98) rendered clearly his dreams of the soul of the legendary dancer-princess, the divine daughter of Herodias."[1] Moreau produced several different versions of this scene, including "Salome dancing before Herod" and "Salome Tattooed," both completed in 1876.]

2. Aubrey Beardsley, Design for the Title Page to the English Edition of *Salome* (1894)

[The image, with its graphic portrayal of the hermaphroditic body, was suppressed in the original but published in the 1907 edition.]

3. Aubrey Beardsley, Final Design for the Title Page (1894)

SALOME

A TRAGEDY IN ONE
ACT : TRANSLATED
FROM THE FRENCH
OF OSCAR WILDE :
PICTURED BY
AUBREY BEARDSLEY

LONDON : ELKIN MATHEWS
& JOHN LANE
BOSTON : COPELAND & DAY
1894

4. Aubrey Beardsley, "The Woman in the Moon" (1894)

[In this image, a face closely resembling Wilde himself appears in the moon, a fact that likely contributed to Wilde's distaste for Beardsley's illustrations (see Introduction, pp. 29-31).]

5. Aubrey Beardsley, "The Climax" (1894)

["The Climax" originally appeared in *The Salon*, prior to the publication of the first English edition of *Salome*. It was this illustration that inspired Wilde to request that Beardsley produce a complete set of images to accompany his play (see Introduction, pp. 29-31).]

Appendix C: Contemporary Responses

1. From Edgar Saltus, *Oscar Wilde: An Idler's Impression* (New York: AMS, 1917), 20

[Wilde reportedly read *Salome* in manuscript to American writer Edgar Saltus (1855-1921), eliciting the following response.]

In his hand was a manuscript, and we were supping on "Salome."

As the banquet proceeded, I experienced that sense of sacred terror which his friends, the Greeks, knew so well. For this thing could have been conceived only by genius wedded to insanity and, at the end, when the tetrarch, rising and bundling his robes about him, cries: "Kill that woman!" the mysterious divinity who the poet may have evoked, deigned perhaps to visit me. For, as I applauded, I shuddered, and told him that I had.

Indifferently he nodded and, assimilating Hugo with superb unconcern, threw out: "It is only the shudder that counts."[1]

2. Pierre Louÿs, "*Salomé*: à Oscar W.," *Pall Mall Budget* (30 June 1892): 947 [my translation]

[The first French edition of *Salome* was dedicated to poet Pierre Louÿs (1870-1925). When Wilde sent a copy to Louÿs, his friend replied in a terse telegram. Wilde was offended and indicated as much in his response to Louÿs, who ultimately made amends by composing the following sonnet.]

Salomé
A Oscar W.

A travers le brouillard lumineux des sept voiles
La courbe de son corps se cambre vers la lune
Elle se touche avec sa chevelure brune
Et ses doigts caressants où luisent des étoiles.

*

---

1 Saltus assumes that Wilde was thinking of how French novelist Victor Hugo (1802-85) responded to the work of Charles Baudelaire (1821-67): "You invest the heaven of art with we know not what deadly rays; you create a new shudder [*un frisson nouveau*]." See Charles Baudelaire, *The Poems and Prose Poems of Charles Baudelaire* (New York: Brentano's, 1919), xxvi.

Le rêve d'être un paon qui déploierait sa queue
La fait sourire sous son éventail de plumes
Elle danse au milieu d'un tourbillon d'écumes
Où flotte l'arc léger de son écharpe bleue.

★

Presque nue, avec son dernier voile, flot jaune,
Elle fuit, revient, tourne, et passe. Au bord du thrône
Le tètrarque tremblant la supplie et l'appelle.

★

Fugitive, qui danse avec des roses soires
Et traîne dans le sang avec ses pieds barbares
L'ombre terrible de la lune derrière elle.

[Translation]

Through the luminous mist of seven veils.
The curve of her body arches to the moon,
She touches herself with her brown hair
And her loving, starlit fingers.

The dream of being a peacock who would display its tail
Makes her smile beneath her fan of feathers
She dances in the middle of a whirlpool of foam
Where the light curve of her blue scarf floats.

Almost naked, with her last veil, yellow stream,
She flees, comes back, turns, and passes. By his throne
The trembling tetrarch begs and calls to her.

Fugitive, who dances with the pink evening
And drags through the blood with her barbaric feet
The terrible shadow of the moon behind her.

3. Letter from Oscar Wilde to Richard Le Gallienne, 22/23 February 1893, *The Complete Letters of Oscar Wilde*, ed. Merlin Holland and Rupert Hart-Davis (New York: Henry Holt and Company, 2000), 552

[Richard Le Gallienne (1866-1947) was a poet, personal friend, and (briefly) lover of Wilde. Their professional relationship seems to have been characterized by mutual admiration, though Le Gallienne published an unsigned review in the *Star* offering somewhat qualified praise for *Salome*.]

My dear Richard,

I have just read the Star, and write to tell you how pleased I am that you, with your fluid artistic temperament, should have glided into the secret of the soul of my poem, swiftly, surely, just as years ago you glided into my heart.

There are of course things I regret, for yourself. Journalism is a terrible cave where the divine become tainted—for a moment only. Why should the young prophet, rising from the well of darkness, be like a "jack in the box"? Why is it that you describe the chill, skeptical, rationalistic Herodias as an "unimaginative worldly creature"? She is far more than that: she is reason in its tragic raiment, reason with its tragic end—and, oh! Richard, why say I am amusing, when Herod hears that in his *royaume* there is one who can make the dead come to life, and (filled with terror at so hideous a prospect) says in his insolence and his fear "That I do not allow. It would be terrible if the dead came back."

But nothing matters much. You have got into the secret chamber of the house in which Salome was fashioned, and I rejoice to think that to you has my secret been revealed, for you are the lover of beauty, and by her much—perhaps over-much—loved and worshipped. Ever yours
Oscar

4. From a Letter from Bernard Shaw to Oscar Wilde, 28 February 1893, *The Complete Letters of Oscar Wilde*, ed. Merlin Holland and Rupert Hart-Davis (New York: Henry Holt and Company, 2000), 554 n2

[Bernard Shaw (1856-1950) and Oscar Wilde, though never close associates, maintained a friendly correspondence and occasionally exchanged work. After receiving and reading a copy of *Lady Windermere's Fan*, Shaw conveyed to Wilde a hope that he would "follow up hard on that trail; for the drama wants building up very badly; and it is clear that your work lies there."[1]]

Salomé is still wandering in her purple raiment in search of me; and I expect her to arrive a perfect outcast, branded with inky stamps, bruised by flinging from hard hands into red prison vans, stifled and contaminated by herding with review books in the World[2] cells, perhaps outraged by some hasty literary pathologist whose haste to lift

---

1   Quoted in *Bernard Shaw: Theatrics. Selected Correspondence of Bernard Shaw*, ed. Dan H. Laurence (Toronto: U of Toronto P, 1995), 9.

2   A society journal founded in 1874 by Grenville Murray and Edmund Yates.

the purple robe blinded him to the private name on the hem. In short, I suspect that they have muddled it up with the other books in York St.;[1] and I have written to them to claim my own.

I have always said that the one way of abolishing the Censor is to abolish the Monarchy of which he is an appendage. But the brute could be lamed if only the critics and authors would make real war on him. The reason they won't is that they are all Puritans at heart. And the coming powers—the proletarian voters—will back their Puritanism unless I can lure the Censor into attacking the political freedom of speech on the stage.

5. From a Letter from Max Beerbohm to Reginald Turner, February 1893, *Letters to Reggie Turner*, ed. Rupert Hart-Davis (London: Lippincott, 1964), 32[2]

The book that they have bound in Parma violets and across whose page is the silver voice of the Master made visible—how could it not be lovely? I am enamoured of it. It has charmed my eyes from their sockets and through the voids has sent incense to my brain: my tongue is loosed in its praise. Have you read it? In construction it is very like a Greek play, I think: yet in conception so modern that its publication in any century would seem premature. It is a marvelous play. If Oscar would re-write *all* the Bible, there would be no sceptics. I say it is a marvelous play. It is a lovely present.

6. From "*Salomé,*" *The Times* (23 February 1893): 8

Of Mr. Oscar Wilde's Salomé: Drame en un Acte (Elkin Mathews and John Lane), we are constrained to express an equally unfavourable opinion.[3] This is the play, written for Mme. Sarah Bernhardt,[4] which the Lord Chamberlain declined to license for performance in this

---

1 In the nineteenth century, York Street was home to several booksellers and publishers.

2 Max Beerbohm (1872-1956) would become famous for his caricatures of Wilde and his circle, but was also a keen admirer of the aesthete. Reginald Turner (1869-1938) was a novelist and member of Wilde's inner circle who continued to support Wilde after his release from prison.

3 The remarks on *Salome* follow, in this article, a similarly negative appraisal of Henrik Ibsen's *The Master Builder* (1892).

4 Wilde encountered Bernhardt (1844-1923) at the home of actor Henry Irving (1838-1905), where she reportedly asked him to write a play for her. Wilde is said to have replied: "I have already done so" (Nick Frankel, "The Dance of Writing: Wilde's *Salomé* as a Work of Contradiction," *Oscar Wilde's Decorated*

country. It is an arrangement in blood and ferocity, morbid, *bizarre*, repulsive, and very offensive in its adaptation of scriptural phraseology to situations the reverse of sacred. It is not ill-suited to some of the less attractive phases of Mme. Bernhardt's dramatic genius, as it is vigorously written in some parts. As a whole, it does credit to Mr. Wilde's command of the French language, but we must say that the opening scene reads to us very like a page from one of Ollendorff's exercises.[1]

7. From a Review of *Salomé*, *Pall Mall Gazette* (27 February 1893): 3

Salomé is a mosaic. Mr. Wilde has many masters, and the influence of each master asserts itself in his pages as stripes of different colours assert themselves in stuffs from the East. The reader of *Salomé* seems to stand in the Island of Voices and to hear around him and about the utterances of friends, the whisperings of demigods. Now it is the voice of Gautier,[2] painting pictures in words of princesses and jewels and flowers and unguents. Anon it is Maeterlinck who speaks—Maeterlinck the Lord of the Low Countries—with his iterations and reiterations, his questions and conundrums, that make so many of his pages—and so many of Mr. Wilde's pages—recall the Book of Riddles that Master Slender sighed for.[3] The chorus seems to be swelled by the speech like silver of Anatole France, perchance by the speech like gold of Marcel Schwob.[4] But the

---

Books, 47-78 [Ann Arbor: U of Michigan P, 2000], 50). When the story was repeated, however, Wilde adamantly denied that he had written the play specifically for Bernhardt: "my play was in no sense of the words written for this great actress. I have never written a play for any actor or actress, nor shall I ever do so. Such work is for the artisan in literature—not for the artist" (*Complete Letters* 336).

1 Heinrich Gottfried Ollendorf (1803-65), a German grammarian, had an enormous impact on language instruction in the nineteenth century.

2 Théophile Gautier (1811-72) was a French poet, novelist, and critic whom Wilde much admired.

3 Maurice Maeterlinck (1862-1949) was a Belgian writer who, though a Fleming, wrote in French and is often cited as a source of stylistic inspiration for Wilde. The reviewer's mention of "the Book of Riddles that Master Slender sighed for" refers to Shakespeare's *The Merry Wives of Windsor* (I.i) and suggests that Wilde, like Slender, is only capable of ventriloquizing the wisdom of others. See Appendix A10, pp. 105-06.

4 Anatole France (1844-1924) was a French writer known for his peculiar blend of eloquence and irony. Marcel Schwob (1867-1905) was the Jewish-French writer to whom Wilde dedicated his poem "The Sphinx" (1894). Schwob was one of the group of French symbolists who commented on early drafts of *Salomé*.

voices that breathe the breath of life into *Salomé* are dominated by one voice, the voice of Flaubert. If Flaubert had not written *Salammbo*,[1] if Flaubert had not written *La Tentation de Saint Antoine*[2]—above all, if Flaubert had not written *Herodias*,[3] *Salomé* might boast an originality to which she cannot now lay claim. She is the daughter of too many fathers. She is a victim of heredity. Her bones want strength, her flesh wants vitality, her blood is polluted. There is no pulse of passion in her ...

There is no freshness in Mr. Wilde's ideas; there is no freshness in his method of presenting those ideas.

8. Letter from Stéphane Mallarmé to Oscar Wilde, March 1893, *Correspondance* 6, Janvier 1893-1894, ed. H. Mondor & L.J. Austin (Paris: Gallimard, 1984), 60 [my translation]

Mon cher poète,

J'admire que tout étant exprimé par de perpétuels traits éblouissants, en votre *Salomé*, il se dégage, aussi, à chaque page de l'indicible et le songe. Ainsi les gemmes innombrables et exactes ne peuvent server que d'accompagnement sur sa robe au geste surnaturel de cette jenue princesse, que définitivement vous évoquâtes.

Amitiés de
Stéphane Mallarmé

My dear poet,

I so admire that in your *Salomé* everything is expressed in continually dazzling strokes, and that also, every page radiates something of the unutterable and the dream. In this way the innumerable, true gems cannot but serve as the accompaniment to the costume of the young princess's supernatural movement, which you have definitively evoked.

With best wishes,
Stéphane Mallarmé

---

1 See Appendix A9, p. 103, note 2.

2 A book by Flaubert published in 1874 and focusing on the temptation of Anthony the Great. Assuming the form of a play script, although never intended for performance, the volume was a favorite of Wilde's. Along with *Salome*, it was one of the books he requested that Robert Ross bring to him during his incarceration at Reading Gaol.

3 A short story by Flaubert, which first appeared in *Trois Contes* (*Three Tales*) in 1877. See Appendix A7, pp. 96-99.

9. From William Archer, "Mr. Oscar Wilde's New Play," *Black and White* (11 May 1893): 290

[William Archer (1856-1924) objected strenuously to the censorship of Wilde's play. Wilde appreciated the review and responded to him directly: "I want to tell you how gratified I was by your letter in the PMG [*Pall Mall Gazette*], not merely for its very courteous and generous recognition of my work, but for its strong protest against the contemptible official tyranny that exists in England in reference to the drama."[1]]

... I have read *Salomé* twice in two hours; in other words, I have added two hours to the tale of that life within our life, which alone, in the long run, is really worth living—the life of the imagination. Hypnotised by the poet—for what is the magic of poetry but a form of hypnotism?—I have lived through what Hilde Wangel would call "the loveliest thing in the world—a drama in the air."[2] A sultry, languorous Syrian night; a sinister moon gliding through the heavens, "like a woman risen from a tomb"; Herod, "with mole-like eyes under quivering lids," gazing at the daughter of his brother's wife, now his own; Herodias, keeping watch on his every glance; Salomé, "pale as the image of a white rose in a mirror of silver"; [...]

Without any scheme, and following no principle of selection, I have jotted down the high lights, as it were, of the picture left on my mind by Mr. Wilde's poem. In speaking of a picture, however, I am not sure that I use the happiest analogy. There is at least as much musical as pictorial quality in *Salomé*. It is by methods borrowed from music that Mr. Wilde, without sacrificing its suppleness, imparts to his prose the firm texture, so to speak, of verse. Borrowed from music—may I conjecture?—through the intermediation of Maeterlinck.[3] Certain it is that the brief melodious phrases, the chiming repetitions, the fugal effects beloved by the Belgian poet, are no less characteristic of Mr. Wilde's method. I am quite willing to believe, if necessary, that the two artists invented their similar devices independently, to meet a common need; but if, as a matter of fact, the one has taken a hint from the other, I do not see that his essential originality is thereby impaired. There is far more depth and body in Mr. Wilde's work than in Maeterlinck's. His characters are men and women, not filmy shapes of mist and moonshine. His properties, so to speak, are far more various and

---

1   *Complete Letters* 534.
2   In Henrik Ibsen's play *The Master Builder* (1892), the companion of Halvard Solness, an architect who promises to build her "castles in the sky."
3   See Appendix A10, pp. 105-06.

less conventional. His palette—I recur, in spite of myself, to the pictorial analogy—is infinitely richer. Maeterlinck paints in washes of water-colour; Mr. Wilde attains the depths and brilliancy of oils. *Salomé* has all the qualities of a great historical picture—pedantry and conventionality excepted.

Its suppression by the Censor was perfectly ridiculous and absolutely inevitable. The censor is the official mouthpiece of Philistinism, and Philistinism would doubtless have been outraged had *Salomé* been represented on the stage. There is not a word in it which can reasonably give pain to the most sensitive Christian; but Philistinism has not yet got rid of the superstition that art is profane, especially the art of acting, and that even to name certain names—and much more to present certain persons—in the theatre, is necessarily to desecrate them. The atmosphere of the play is certainly none of the healthiest; but if an artist sets forth to paint a fever jungle, we can scarcely complain if his picture be not altogether breezy and exhilarating.

10. From Lord Alfred Douglas, "*Salomé*: A Critical Overview," *The Spirit Lamp* 4.1 (Oxford: James Thornton, 1893)

[Douglas (1870-1945) wrote this piece shortly after completing his English translation of the play. In 1918, he expressed "regret" at having contributed to the production of what he deemed "a most pernicious and abominable piece of work."[1]]

That mouthpiece of Philistinism the daily press, surpassed itself in the stern and indignant condemnation of the book which it had not read and the play which it had not seen; never before it declared had such an outrage on decency and good taste been committed, never had a more infamous plot against morality and the Bible been nipped in the bud. For it *was* nipped in the bud, the censor had refused to license its production, England was saved from lasting disgrace. The daily press positively swelled with pride, it metaphorically slapped its chest and thanked God it was an Englishman. It is hard to understand the attitude taken up by the anonymous scribblers who propounded these pompous absurdities. Why it should be taken for granted that because a writer takes his subject from a sublime and splendid literature, he should necessarily treat it in a contemptible manner, is a mystery it is hard to solve. Apparently it never occurred to these enlightened beings

---

1 Verbatim Report 291. See Appendix E15, p. 148.

that the very sublimity and grandeur of such a subject would be a sufficient guarantee that the artist had put his very best work into it, and had done his utmost to exalt his treatment to the high level his subject demanded. To a man who takes for the scene of a vulgar farce, the back drawing-room of a house in Bloomsbury,[1] and who brings on to the stage a swindling stockbroker or a rag-and-bone merchant, they are ready to listen with delighted attention, to laugh at his coarse jokes and revel in his cockney dialogue; good healthy English fun they call it. But a man who actually takes for the scene of a tragedy the gorgeous background of a Roman Tetrarch's court, and who brings on to the stage a real prophet out of the Bible, and all in French too! "No, it is too much," they say, "we don't want to hear anything more about it, it is an outrage and an infamy." O Happy England, land of healthy sentiment, roast beef and Bible, long may you have such men to keep guard over your morals, to point out to you the true path, and to guide your feet into the way of cant! [...]

One thing strikes one very forcibly in the treatment, the musical form of it. Again and again it seems to one that in reading one is *listening*; listening, not to the author, not to the direct unfolding of a plot, but to the tones of different instruments, suggesting, suggesting, always indirectly, till one feels that by shutting one's eyes one can best catch the suggestion. The author's personality nowhere shews itself.[2]

The French is as much Mr. Wilde's own as is the psychological motive of the play, it is perfect in scholarship, but it takes a form new in French literature. It is a daring experiment and a complete success. The language is rich and coloured, but never precious, and shows a command of expression so full and varied that the ascetically artistic restraint of certain passages stands out in strong relief. Such a passage is the one quoted above: the conversation of the soldiers on the terrace; in which by-the-bye certain intelligent critics have discovered a resemblance to Ollendorf,[3] and with extraordinary shallowness and lack of artistic sensibility have waxed facetious over. O wonderful men!

Artistically speaking the play would gain nothing by performance, to my mind it would lose much. To be appreciated it must be abstracted, and to be abstracted it must be read. Let it, "not to the

---

1 Bloomsbury is a London neighborhood which, in the nineteenth century, was home to many middle-class professionals, including Charles Dickens, William Makepeace Thackeray, Anthony Trollope, and several members of the Pre-Raphaelite Brotherhood.

2 In his preface to *The Picture of Dorian Gray*, Wilde writes: "To reveal art and conceal the artist is art's aim" (48).

3 See Appendix C6, p. 117, note 1.

sensual ear but more endeared, pipe to the spirit ditties of no tone."[1]

It only remains to say that the treatment of St. John the Baptist is perfectly refined and reverend.

I suppose the play is unhealthy, morbid, unwholesome, and un-English, ça va sans dire.[2] It is certainly un-English, because it is written in French, and therefore unwholesome to the average Englishman, who can't digest French. It is probably morbid and unhealthy, for there is no representation of quiet domestic life, nobody slaps anybody else on the back all through the play, and there is not a single reference to Christianity, there are no muscular Christians.[3] Anyone, therefore, who suffers from that most appalling and widespread of diseases which takes the form of a morbid desire for health had better avoid and flee from Salomé, or they will surely get a shock that it will take months of the daily papers and Charles Kingsley's novels to counteract. But the less violently and aggressively healthy, those who are healthy to live and do not live to be healthy, will find in Mr. Oscar Wilde's tragedy the beauty of a perfect work of art, a joy for ever, ambrosia to feed their souls with honey of sweet-bitter thoughts.

---

1 From John Keats, "Ode on a Grecian Urn" (1819).

2 Douglas's use of the French phrase—which translates as "That goes without saying"—is playful and ironic given his critique of "the average Englishman, who can't digest French."

3 Muscular Christianity was a model of masculinity, made especially popular in the nineteenth century by Charles Kingsley (1819-75), which stresses the importance of combining devout religious practice with the cultivation of physical health.

Appendix D: Translation History

[Wilde originally composed *Salome* in French, observing at one point that he was inspired by the "curious effect" that the Belgian playwright Maurice Maeterlinck produced by writing "in an alien language" (Mikhail 1: 188). When Wilde decided to publish an English edition of *Salome*, he recruited Lord Alfred Douglas for the task. The fact that *Salome* has since been translated into several languages (including German, Czech, Hebrew, Dutch, Greek, Italian, Polish Russian, Spanish, Catalan, Swedish, and Yiddish) reflects the play's concern with the plasticity of language; however, it has also presented obstacles for readers and scholars.

Douglas's translation, which omits important details and is occasionally inaccurate (see Appendix D6, pp. 126-30), has been a source of much controversy. Wilde himself was critical of Douglas's translation and eventually amended it, although the extent of his alterations remains somewhat difficult to assess. This collaboration between Douglas and Wilde constituted the first English edition of the play and, because it is the only English translation overseen by Wilde, it is the translation used in this volume.]

1. Letter from Lord Alfred Douglas to John Lane, 30 September 1893 (MS Div. Rosenbach Museum and Library)

[Douglas's translation, which Wilde felt to be on several points flawed, led to a disagreement between the two men. After heated argument, Douglas withdrew from work on the edition.]

Dear Lane,

Oscar and I have found it impossible to agree about the translation of certain passages, phrases and words in *Salome*, and consequently as I cannot consent to have my work altered and edited, and thus to become a mere machine for doing the rough work of translation, I have decided to relinquish the affair altogether.

You and Oscar can therefore arrange between you as to who the translator is to be. My private opinion is that unless Oscar translates it himself, he will not be satisfied.

Yours very truly
Alfred Douglas

2. From a Letter from Lord Alfred Douglas to John Lane, 16 November 1893 (MS Div. Rosenbach Museum and Library)

[Rather than identifying Douglas as the translator, Wilde dedicated the first English edition of the play to him. Apparently, Douglas was at least somewhat appeased by the gesture.]

In the meanwhile let me assure you that nothing would have induced me to sanction the publication of *Salome* without my name on the title-page (and the matter was left entirely in my hands by Mr Wilde), if I had not been persuaded that the dedication which is to be made to me is of infinitely greater artistic & literary value, than the appearance of my name on the title-page. It was only a few days ago that I fully realized that the difference between the dedication of *Salome* to me by the author and the appearance of my name on the title-page is the difference between a tribute to admiration from an artist and a receipt from a tradesman.

3. From a Letter from Oscar Wilde to Lord Alfred Douglas, January-March 1897, *The Complete Letters of Oscar Wilde*, ed. Merlin Holland and Rupert Hart-Davis (New York: Henry Holt and Company, 2000), 682

[This excerpt is taken from the letter that, once transcribed and revised by Robert Ross, would be published as *De Profundis*. In total, the letter consists of 20 folio sheets, which were written intermittently during Wilde's incarceration at Reading Gaol.]

Three months later still, in September new scenes occurred, the occasion of them being my pointing out the schoolboy faults of your attempted translation of *Salomé*. You must by this time be a fair enough French scholar to know that the translation was as unworthy of you, as an ordinary Oxonian, as it was of the work it sought to render. You did not of course know it then, and in one of the violent letters you wrote to me on the point you said that you were under "*no intellectual obligation of any kind*" to me. I remember that when I read that statement, I felt that it was the one really true thing you had written to me in the whole course of our friendship. I saw that a less cultivated nature would really have suited you much better. I am not saying this in bitterness at all, but simply as a fact of companionship. Ultimately the bond of all companionship, whether in marriage or in friendship, is conversation, and conversation must have a common basis, and between two people of widely different culture the only common basis possible is the lowest level. The trivial in thought and action is charming. I had made it the keystone of a very brilliant philosophy expressed in plays and paradoxes. But the froth and folly of our life grew often very wearisome to me: it was only in the mire that we met [...]

4. From a Letter from Robert Ross to Frank Harris, undated, Frank Harris, *Oscar Wilde: His Life and Confessions* (New York: Brentano's, 1916), 608n

[Robert Ross (1869-1918) objected strongly to Douglas's translation of the play and, in this letter to Frank Harris (1856-1931)—Irish-born author, editor, journalist, and publisher who knew and admired Wilde—indicates that his own translation of the text quietly replaced that of Douglas in the 1905, 1906, and 1912 editions.]

Do you happen to have compared Douglas' translation of Salome in Lane's First edition (with Beardsley's illustrations) with Lane's Second edition (with Beardsley's illustrations) or Lane's little editions (without Beardsley's illustrations)? Or have you ever compared the aforesaid First edition with the original? Douglas' translation omits a great deal of the text and is actually wrong as a rendering of the text in many cases. I have had this out with a good many people. I believe Douglas is to this day sublimely unconscious that his text, of which there were never more than 500 copies issued in England, has been entirely scrapped; his name at my instance was removed from the current issues for the very good reason that the new translation is not his. But this is merely an observation not a correction.

5. From Lord Alfred Douglas, *Autobiography* (Freeport, NY: Books for Libraries Press, [1929] 1970), 160n

[Douglas's 1929 *Autobiography* provides a very different account of the play's translation history. In a lengthy footnote, Douglas suggests that Wilde originally drafted the play in English and only later, and with a great deal of help from André Gide and Pierre Louÿs, was able to produce the French text. The accounts of Wilde's French associates, including Gide and Louÿs, contradict Douglas's claim. The manuscript currently held at the Rosenbach Museum and Library (Philadelphia) reveals that the corrections recommended by Louÿs pertain chiefly to matters of punctuation, reflexive verbs, and other minor points of grammar. Moreover, while Beardsley did (as Douglas suggests) offer to translate the play, no such translation has surfaced to validate the claim that he actually produced a manuscript, only to have Wilde reject it.]

When I had finished the translation, to which I devoted a great deal of time and careful work, Oscar did not like it. In fact he actually yielded to the solicitations of Aubrey Beardsley, who declared that he could do a splendid translation and that he thoroughly understood the spirit of the play, and who begged Oscar to let him do it. I was, not unnaturally, somewhat offended at this, and was rather gratified, I must confess, when a month later, after Oscar had received and read Beardsley's translation, he declared that it was "utterly hopeless," and that he would, on second thoughts, rather have mine, the manuscript of which I had meanwhile taken back. I told Oscar that if my translation was any use to him he could use it, and that anything in it he did not like he could alter. But I added that if he altered it, it would no longer be my translation, and that in that case it would not be advisable for my name to appear as the translator. Oscar used my translation, making a few alterations. Really I believe he originally wrote the play in English and translated it into French with the assistance of Pierre Louÿs and André Gide. So that to get anyone at all to "translate" it was a rather ridiculous pose. At the time Oscar wrote this play he did not know French well enough to write a play in the language, and André Gide told me later that Oscar's first draft was a mass of blunders and misspelling. Pierre Louÿs and he knocked it into shape, and when it came to a translation into English, Oscar just put it back more or less into his own original language, altering my translation where it differed from his own words. Consequently I do not regard the present translation, which is usually attributed to me, and which is dedicated to me as the translator, as mine at all. I do not claim it as my translation. I think my own translation, as a matter of fact, was much better!

6. Translation Chart

[The following chart indicates differences between Wilde's original French text and the translations offered by Lord Alfred Douglas, Robert Ross, and Richard Ellmann. In order to highlight some of the more striking discrepancies, annotations have been provided in the "Commentary" column to the far right.]

Wilde (French)	Douglas (1893)	Ross (1912)	Ellmann (1982)	Commentary
[Stage direction] Clair de lune.	The moon is shining very brightly. (p. 47)	Moonlight. (719)	A full moon. (293)	[Stage direction] Ross offers the most literal translation. Technically, "clair de lune" indicates moonlight, though not necessarily the light of a full moon ("pleine lune").
Iokanaan. Quand il viendra la terre déserte se réjouira. Elle fleurira comme le lis.	When he cometh, the solitary places shall be glad. They shall blossom like the rose. (p. 50)	When he cometh, the solitary places shall be glad. They shall blossom like the lily. (720)	When he comes, the barren earth will rejoice. It will blossom like the lily. (295)	The French "lis" translates directly as "lily," though in his translation Douglas substitutes the very different image of the "rose." Ross and Ellmann provide the more accurate translation—one that preserves a reference to the British aesthetes.
The Cappadocian. Une ancienne citerne! Cela doit être très malsain.	An old cistern! That must be a poisonous place in which to dwell! (p. 51)	An old cistern ! It must be very unhealthy. (721)	An old cistern! It must be full of disease. (297)	Douglas frequently adds extra words to his translation, thus departing at times from the brevity and cadence of Wilde's French. The most literal translation, provided by Ross, thus preserves not only the meaning but also the cadence of the original French text.
Salomé. Pourqui le tétrarque me regarde-t-il toujours avec ses yeux de taupe sous ses paupières tremblantes?	Why does the Tetrarch look at me all the while with his mole's eyes under his shaking eyelids? (p. 52)	Why does the Tetrarch look at me all the while with his mole's eyes under his shaking eyelids? (721)	Why does the tetrarch keep looking at me with those mole's eyes under his quivering eyelids? (298)	Douglas, Ross, and Ellmann translate the phrase "ses yeux de taupe" literally as "his mole's eyes." Consequently, as Anne Margaret Daniel suggests, English translations of the text risk overlooking the color pun conveyed by the original French.[1]

---

1 For an illuminating account of the work's translation history, see Anne Margaret Daniel's "Lost in Translation: Oscar, Bosie, and *Salomé*," *Princeton University Library Chronicle* 68.1-2 (2006 Autumn-2007 Winter): 60-70. See also Rodney Shewan, "Oscar Wilde's *Salomé*: A Critical Variorum Edition," Ph.D. dissertation (University of Reading, 1982).

Wilde (French)	Douglas (1893)	Ross (1912)	Ellmann (1982)	Commentary
The Page of Herodias. Pourquoi lui parler? Pourquoi la regarder? Oh! il va arriver un malheur.	Why do you speak to her? Oh! something terrible will happen. Why do you look at her? (p. 52)	Why do you speak to her? Why do you look at her? Oh! something terrible will happen. (721)	Why speak to her? Why look at her? . . . Oh! something terrible is about to happen. (298)	Occasionally, as in this instance, Douglas rearranges the order of Wilde's sentences. In his translation, Ross reverts to the original order.
Iokanaan. Il est venu, le Seigneur! Il est venu le fils de l'Homme. Les centaures se sont cachés dans les rivières, et les sirènes ont quitté les rivières et couchent sous les feuilles dans les forêts.	Behold! The Lord hath come. The Son of Man is at hand. The centaures have hidden themselves in the rivers, and the nymphs have left the rivers, and are lying beneath the leaves in the forests. (p. 53)	The Lord hath come. The Son of Man hath come. The centaures have hidden themselves in the rivers, and the sirens have left the rivers, and are lying beneath the leaves in the forests. (722)	The Lord hath come. The Son of Man hath come. The centaurs have hidden in the rivers, and the sirens have left the rivers and lie under the leaves of the forest. (298)	Here, Douglas again introduces Scriptural language ("Behold!") that does not appear in the original. Moreover, he translates the French "les sirènes" as "nymphs." Whereas nymphs were female nature deities, the sirens are femmes fatales whose seductive voices would lure unsuspecting sailors to their deaths. Because the sirens call upon a very specific mythology, the restoration of the term "siren" in the versions of Ross and Ellmann is significant.
Herodias. Cet homme vomit toujours des injures contre moi.	This man is for ever hurling insults at me. (p. 66)	This man is for ever vomiting insults against me. (729)	This man is for ever vomiting insults against me. (311)	Douglas's decision to translate "vomit" as "hurl" is fitting in contemporary English, though Ross and Ellmann reinforce Wilde's corporeal language by offering a more literal translation. Vyvyan Holland substitutes the phrase "spews out" in his 1957 translation (Holland 37).

Iokanaan. Que les capitaines de guerre la percent de leurs épées, qu'ils l'écrasent sous leurs boucliers.	Let the captains of the hosts pierce her with their swords, let them crush her beneath their shields. (p. 71)	Let the war captains pierce her with their swords, let them crush her beneath their shields. (732)	Let the captains of the hosts pierce her with their swords, let them crush her beneath their shields. (316)	The phrase "capitaines de guerre" translates literally (as indicated in Ross's edition) as "war captains." Douglas and Ellmann choose "captains of the host," a phrase that carries decidedly Scriptural connotations, as it is a term used to denote leaders of God's legion.
Herod. Oh! on dirait qu'il y a un oiseau, un grand oiseau noir, qui plane sur la terrasse.	Ah! one might fancy a huge black bird that hovers over the terrace. (p. 76)	Ah! One might fancy a bird, a huge black bird that hovers over the terrace. (735)	Oh! it might be a bird, a huge black bird which hovers over the terrace. (321)	At times, Douglas omits phrases that are repeated, even though this was a device that Wilde borrowed from Maeterlinck and deliberately cultivated in the French. Ross and Ellmann restore the repetition in the phrase "a bird, a huge black bird."
Herod. Il ne faut pas trouver des symbols dans chaque chose qu'on voit. Cela rend la vie impossible.	It is not wise to find symbols in everything that one sees. It makes life too full of terrors. (p. 76)	You must not find symbols in everything you see. It makes life impossible. (735)	We must not find symbols in everything we see. To do so would make life impossible. (321)	Once again Douglas's translation does not correspond strictly to the original French. As the translations of Ross and Ellmann indicate, "impossible" is the more literal translation, as opposed to "full of terrors," which would more closely correspond to the French phrase "pleine de terreur."
Herod. Il a prédit que la lune deviendrait rouge comme du sang.	He prophesied that the moon would become as blood. (p. 77)	He prophesied that the moon would become red as blood. (736)	He prophesied that the moon would become red like blood. (323)	Occasionally, Douglas omits color detail. In this particular case, Ross and Ellmann restore the color to Wilde's simile, "rouge comme du sang" ("red as blood").

Wilde (French)	Douglas (1893)	Ross (1912)	Ellmann (1982)	Commentary
Herodias. Je le vois bien, et les étoiles tombent comme des figues vertes, n'est-ce pas?	Oh yes, I see it well, and the stars are falling like unripe figs, are they not? (p. 77)	Oh yes, I see it well, and the stars are falling like ripe figs, are they not? (736)	I see it well enough, and the stars fall like green figs, do they not? (323)	Douglas and Ross differ on the question of whether green figs are ripe or unripe. In this case, Ellmann returns to the term used in Sacy's Bible, which is also consistent with Wilde's appeal to color throughout the text: "figues vertes."
Herod. Je n'ai jamais été dur envers vous.	I have ever been kind toward thee. (p. 79)	I have never been hard to you. (737)	I have never been harsh with you. (325)	Douglas's departure from the negative construction provided in the original French substantively alters the meaning of the text. To be kind is hardly equivalent to not being cruel, and Douglas's translation introduces a slightly different characterization of Herod's relationship to Salome, which both Ross and Ellmann revise.
Salomé. Derrière tes mains et tes blasphèmes tu as caché ton visage.	With the cloak of thine hands, and with the cloak of thy blasphemies thou didst hide thy face. (p. 84)	Behind thine hands and thy curses thou didst hide thy face. (741)	You hid your face behind your hands and your blasphemies. (330)	Here, Douglas represents Iokanaan's hands and face metaphorically as "cloaks," a figuration that is not in the original text.

Appendix E: Performance History

[By June 1892, rehearsals of *Salome* were already under way at the Palace Theatre. Rehearsals ceased when the play was banned by the Lord Chamberlain. This unrealized production was the only one Wilde would ever have a hand in shaping, but the following documents help to illustrate what this original performance might have looked like.]

1. From Charles Ricketts, *Self Portrait* (London: P. Davies, 1939), 137

[Artist and writer Charles Ricketts (1866-1931) was commissioned to design the set for the original performance of *Salome*. His vision seems to reflect Wilde's attention to color in the text of the play.]

I proposed a black floor, upon which Salome's feet could move like white doves; this was said to capture the author. The sky was to be a rich turquoise green, cut by the perpendicular fall of gilded strips of Japanese matting forming an aerial tent above the terraces. Did Wilde suggest the division of the actors into separate masses of colour? To-day I cannot decide. The Jews were to be in yellow, John in white, and Herod and Herodias in blood-red. Over Salome the discussions were endless; Should she be clothed in black—like the night, in silver like the moon or—the suggestion was Wilde's—green like a curious poisonous lizard.

2. From Graham Robertson, *Time Was* (London: Hamilton, 1931), 125-26

[Graham Robertson (1866-1948) designed the costumes for the original production of *Salome* at the request of Sarah Bernhardt. Both Robertson and Wilde expressed a desire that the wardrobe represent varying shades of yellow. According to Stanley Weintraub, "yellow was not only the decor of the notorious and dandified pre-Victorian Regency, but also of the allegedly wicked and decadent French novel."[1] Thus, we might speculate that the choice of yellow reflects Wilde's investment in the French cultural context from which the play itself emerged.]

---

1   Stanley Weintraub, *The Yellow Book: Quintessence of the Nineties* (New York: Doubleday, 1964), 99.

"I should like," he [Wilde] said, throwing off the notion, I believe, at random, "I should like everyone on the stage to be in yellow."

It was a good idea and I saw its possibilities at once—every costume of some shade of yellow—from clearest lemon to deep orange, with here and there just a hint of black ... and all upon a pale ivory terrace against a great empty sky of deepest violet. "A violet sky," repeated Oscar Wilde slowly. "Yes—I never thought of that. Certainly a violet sky and then, in place of an orchestra, braziers of perfume. Think—the scented clouds rising and partly veiling the stage from time to time—a new perfume for each emotion!"

"Ye-es," said I doubtfully, "but you couldn't air the theatre between each emotion, and the perfumes would get mixed and smell perfectly beastly and—no, I don't think I care for the perfume idea, but the yellow scheme is splendid."

3. Photograph of Sarah Bernhardt in Costume as Salome, 1891, by Napoléon Sarony

[Sarah Bernhardt (1844-1923) was a world-renowned French stage actress. In her autobiography, *My Double Life* (1907), Bernhardt recalled her first encounter with Wilde, who joined a throng of devotees upon her arrival in London in 1879. Wilde apparently tossed a bouquet of lilies at her feet, as Bernhardt recalls:

I stopped short, rather confused, not daring to walk on these white flowers, but the crowd pressing on behind compelled me to advance, and the poor lilies had to be trodden under foot.

"Hip, hip, hurrah! A cheer for Sarah Bernhardt!" shouted the turbulent young man.

His head was above all the other heads; he had luminous eyes and long hair, and looked like a German student. He was an English poet, though, and one of the greatest of the century, a poet who was a genius, but who was, alas! later tortured and finally vanquished by madness. It was Oscar Wilde.[1]]

---

1   Sarah Bernhardt, *My Double Life: Memoirs of Sarah Bernhardt* (London: William Heinemann, 1907), 197-98.

SARA BERNHARDT.

COPYRIGHT, 1891, BY NAPOLEON SARONY.

87 UNION SQR. N. Y.

4. From a Letter from Oscar Wilde to William Rothenstein, July 1892, *The Complete Letters of Oscar Wilde*, ed. Merlin Holland and Rupert Hart-Davis (New York: Henry Holt and Company, 2000), 531-33

[The Lord Chamberlain, who by the Licensing Act of 1737 was responsible for overseeing censorship of the theater, banned the public performance of *Salome* on the grounds that it was blasphemous to represent biblical subjects on the stage. The Examiner of Plays, Edward F. Smyth Pigott, may have been motivated by other objections. In a private letter, he suggested that the play's sexual undertones played a role in his decision, calling it "a miracle of impudence" and noting that Salome's "love turns to fury because John will not let her kiss him *in the mouth*—and in the last scene, where she brings in his head—if you please—on a 'charger'—she *does* kiss his mouth, in a paroxysm of sexual despair. The piece is written in French—half Biblical, half pornographic—by Oscar Wilde himself."[1] The ban would remain in effect until 1931.]

The licenser of plays is nominally the Lord Chamberlain, but really a commonplace official—in the present case a Mr Pigott, who panders to the vulgarity and hypocrisy of the English people, by licensing every low farce and vulgar melodrama. He even allows the stage to be used for the purpose of the caricaturing of the personalities of artists, and at the same moment when he prohibited *Salome*, he licensed a burlesque of *Lady Windermere's Fan*[2] in which an actor dressed up like me and imitated my voice and manner!!![3] The curious thing is this: all the arts are free in England, except the actor's art; it is held by the Censor that the stage degrades and that actors desecrate fine subjects, so the Censor prohibits not the publication of *Salome* but its production. Yet not one single actor has protested against this insult to the stage—not even [Henry] Irving, who is always prating about the Art of the Actor. This shows how few actors are artists. All the *dramatic* critics, except Archer of the *World*,[4] agree with the Censor that there should be a censorship over actors and acting! This shows how bad our stage must be, and also shows how Philistine the English journalists are.

I am very ill, dear Will, and can't write any more. Ever yours,

Oscar Wilde

---

1 Quoted in John Russell Stephens, *The Censorship of English Drama, 1824-1901* (Cambridge: Cambridge UP, 2012), 112.

2 Wilde's incredibly successful play, first staged in 1892 at the St. James's Theatre, London.

3 Refers to *The Poet and the Puppets*, a farce produced by Charles Brookfield and J.M. Glover, which pointedly mocks the mannerisms and character of Wilde.

4 See Appendix C9, pp. 119-120.

5. "Mr. Oscar Wilde on *Salome*," *The Times* (2 March 1893): 4

To the Editor of the Times.

Sir, My attention has been drawn to a review of "Salomé" which was published in your columns last week.[1] The opinions of English critics on a French work of mine have, of course, little, if any interest for me. I write simply to ask you to allow me to correct a misstatement that appears in the review in question.

The fact that the greatest tragic actress of any stage now living saw in my play such beauty that she was anxious to produce it, to take herself the part of the heroine, to lend the entire poem the glamour of her personality, and to my prose the music of her flute-like voice—this was naturally, and always will be, a source of pride and pleasure to me, and I look forward with delight to seeing Mme. Bernhardt present my play in Paris, that vivid centre of art, where religious dramas are often performed. But my play was in no sense of the words written for this great actress. I have never written a play for any actor or actress, nor shall I ever do so. Such work is for the artisan in literature—not for the artist.

I remain, Sir, your obedient servant

Oscar Wilde

6. From Oscar Wilde, "The Censure and *Salome*," *Pall Mall Budget* 40 (30 June 1892): 947

[Robert Ross conducted an interview with Wilde regarding the censorship of the play for the *Pall Mall Budget*, a portion of which is reproduced here. Ross was a former lover and lifelong friend of Wilde's, serving as the writer's executor after his death. For the 1930 edition of *Salome* published by John Lane, Ross wrote an introductory note detailing the production and performance of the play, noting that "*Salomé* has made the author's name a household word wherever the English language is not spoken," a remark that reflects the stark contrast between English censorship of the play and the success of *Salome* in theaters across Europe at the beginning of the twentieth century.[2]]

Personally to have my *première* in Paris instead of in London is a great honour, and one that I appreciate sincerely. The pleasure and pride that I have experienced in the whole affair has been that Madame Sarah Bernhardt, who is undoubtedly the greatest artist on any stage,

---

1 See Appendix C6, pp. 116-17.
2 Ross xiii.

should have been charmed and fascinated by my play and should have wished to act it.

Every rehearsal has been a source of intense pleasure to me. To hear my own words spoken by the most beautiful voice in the world has been the greatest artistic joy that it is possible to experience. So that you see, as far as I am concerned, I care very little about the refusal of the Lord Chamberlain to allow my play to be produced. What I do care about is this—that the Censorship apparently regards the stage as the lowest of all the arts, and looks on acting as a vulgar thing. The painter is allowed to take his subjects where he chooses. He can go to the great Hebrew and Hebrew-Greek literature of the Bible and can paint Salomé dancing or Christ on the Cross or the Virgin with her Child. Nobody interferes with the painter. Nobody says, "Painting is such a vulgar art that you must not paint sacred things." The sculptor is equally free. He can carve St. John the Baptist in his camel hair, and fashion the Madonna or Christ in bronze or in marble as he wills. Yet nobody says to him, "Sculpture is such a vulgar art that you must not carve sacred things." And the writer, the poet—he also is quite free. I can write about any subject I choose. For me there is no Censorship. I can take any incident I like out of sacred literature and treat it as I choose and there is no one to say to the poet, "Poetry is such a vulgar art that you must not use it in treating sacred subjects." But there is a Censorship over the stage and acting; and the basis of that Censorship is that, while vulgar subjects may be put on the stage and acted, while everything that is mean and low and shameful in life can be portrayed by actors, no actor is to be permitted to present under artistic conditions the great and ennobling subjects taken from the Bible. The insult in the suppression of "Salomé" is an insult to the stage as a form of art and not to me.

I shall publish "Salomé." No one has the right to interfere with me, and no one shall interfere with me. The people who are injured are the actors; the art that is vilified is that art of acting. I hold that this is as fine as any other art, and to refuse it the right to treat great and noble subjects is an insult to the stage. The action of the Censorship in England is odious and ridiculous. What can be said of a body that forbids Massenet's *Hérodiade*, Gounod's *La Reine de Saba*, Rubinstein's *Judas Maccabaeus*, and allows *Divorçons* to be placed on any stage?[1] The artistic treatment of moral and elevating subjects is discouraged, while a free course is given to the representation of disgusting and revolting subjects.

---

1 Jules Massenet's 1881 operatic adaptation of Gustave Flaubert's "Hérodias" and Charles Gounod's *La Reine de Saba* (*The Queen of Sheba*) are both examples of successfully staged operas featuring biblical themes. Anton Rubinstein, who composed *Judas Maccabaeus*, wrote several Biblical operas. All of the pre-

My idea of writing the play was simply this: I have one instrument that I know that I can command, and that is the English language. There was another instrument to which I had listened all my life, and I wanted once to touch this new instrument to see whether I could make any beautiful thing out of it. The play was written in Paris some six months ago, where I read it to some young poets who admired it immensely. Of course there are modes of expression that a Frenchman of letters would not have used, but they give a certain relief or colour to the play. A great deal of the curious effect that Maeterlinck produces comes from the fact that he, a Flamand by race, writes in an alien language. The same thing is true of Rossetti who, though he wrote in English, was essentially Latin in temperament.[1]

If the Censor refuses "Salomé," I shall leave England and settle in France where I will take out letters of naturalization. I will not consent to call myself a citizen of a country that shows such narrowness in its artistic judgment. I am not English. I am Irish—which is quite another thing.

A few weeks ago I met Madame Sarah Bernhardt at Mr. Henry Irving's.[2] She had heard of my play and asked me to read it to her. I did so, and she at once expressed a wish to play the *title-rôle*. Of course it has been a great disappointment to her and to her company not to have played this piece in London. We have been rehearsing for three weeks. The costumes, scenery and everything have been prepared, and we are naturally disappointed. Still, all are looking forward now to producing it for the first time in Paris, where the actor is appreciated and the stage is regarded as an artistic medium. It is remarkable how little art there is in the work of dramatic critics in England. You find column after column of description, but the critics rarely know how to praise an artistic work. The fact is, it requires an artist to praise art: any one can pick it to pieces. For my own part, I don't know which I despise most, blame or praise. The latter, I think, for it generally happens that the qualities praised are those which one regards with the least satisfaction oneself.

What makes the Lord Chamberlain's action to me most contemptible—and the only point in which I feel at all aggrieved in the matter—is that he allows the personality of an artist to be presented in a caricature on the stage, and will not allow the work of that artist to be shown under very rare and very beautiful conditions.

---

ceding were banned by the Lord Chamberlain. Victorien Sardou's *Divorçons* (*Let's Get a Divorce*), which follows the story of a woman who attempts to divorce her husband in order to marry a handsome rake, was not suppressed.

1 Dante Gabriel Rossetti, English painter and poet especially known for co-founding the Pre-Raphaelite Brotherhood in 1848. Both of Rossetti's parents were Italian by birth.

2 Famous English actor and manager of the Lyceum Theatre, who was also reputed to be Wilde's favorite performer.

7. Bernard Partridge, "A Wilde Idea," *Punch Magazine* (9 July 1892): 1

[In an interview with Robert Ross, Wilde famously announced that he would become a French citizen in order to protest the Lord Chamberlain's decision.[1] The remark inspired several visual satires, including Bernard Partridge's cartoon for *Punch Magazine*. Here, Wilde is no longer dressed in the fashionable attire for which he had become known. Instead, he dons the costume of a French conscript. With a copy of *Salome* peeking out from his bag, Wilde is represented as a turncoat—a somewhat languorous and dubious soldier waging a cultural war against England.]

---

1 See Appendix E6, pp. 135-37.

8. From a Letter from Max Beerbohm to Reginald Turner, June 1892 (Beerbohm, *Letters* 22)

[In the following passage, Beerbohm imagines satirizing the suppression of Wilde's play in a scene depicting Britain as Herod and the disapproving Mrs. Grundy as Salome. Instead of dancing for the head of John the Baptist, Grundy calls for the condemnation of "Oscar the Poetast," whose mysterious utterances are as disturbing to the censors as the prophecies of Iokanaan are to Herodias and the Jews.]

Isn't it killing about Oscar's *Salome* being interdicted by the Lord Chamberlain. I have designed a great picture in which King Bull[1] makes a great feast and when they have feasted the daughter of Mrs Grundy[2] dances before them and pleases the King—insomuch that he promises her whatsoever she shall desire. After consultation with her mother she demands that "they bring unto her by and by the head of Oscar the Poetast[3] on a charger.

9. Oscar Wilde, "Plan de la scene" (1891)

[The following image, sketched in Wilde's hand, is included at the very beginning of the manuscript of *Salome* currently housed at the Rosenbach Museum and Library. Wilde imagines a stairway ("escalier") in the foreground at downstage right, composing part of the building ("batiment" [*sic*]). A balcony ("balcon") partially overhangs the majority of the scene, with an entranceway ("ouverture") placed upstage right. The moon ("la lune") is placed aloft in the background at upstage center. Whereas Wilde seems originally to have placed Iokanaan's cistern to centerstage left, a second hand recommends moving it to a more central position and thus in closer alignment with the moon itself. The same hand seems to have preferred placing the building and stairway on the opposite side of the stage. Joseph Donohue suggests that these revisions were likely introduced by Charles Ricketts, who was asked to design the set for the original per-

---

1 John Bull has long served as a personification of Britain, often assuming the form of a portly and well-to-do gentleman.
2 A personification of conventional, pedantic, and prudish decorum.
3 A contemptuous name for a writer of mediocre verse; more commonly spelled "poetaster."

formance of *Salome* and "appears to have used this sketch for his own London production" in 1906.[1]]

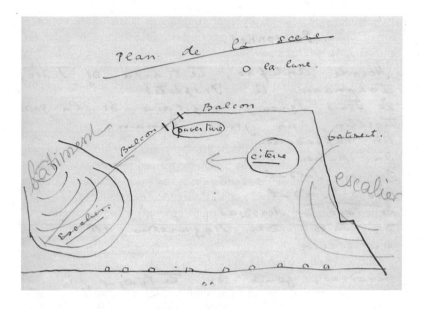

10. From M.J. du Tillet, "Théâtres" [review of the Paris premiere of *Salome*], *Revue bleue politique et littéraire* 4/5 (1896): 218 [my translation]

[The Paris premiere of *Salome* met with mixed reviews. The following excerpt expresses admiration for the play while also suggesting that it has been unduly acclaimed due to growing public sympathy for the incarcerated playwright.]

Le gros événement de la soirée était la representation de *Salomé* de M. Oscar Wilde ... Je parlais tout à l'heure de la prétention naturelle de ces littérateurs exaltés et ingénus; ils sont fermement convaincus que la représentation de *Salomé*, hâtera la libération de l'auteur, emprisonné à la suite de ce que vous savez. Je n'ai pas une confiance absolue ... Parlons donc de *Salomé*, comme si nous n'étions pas responsables de la liberté d'un prisonnier.

---

1 Joseph Donohue, *Plays*, in *The Complete Works of Oscar Wilde*, vol. 5 (Oxford: Oxford UP, 2013), 508; Appendix E1, p. 131.

Je ne sais trop quel nom conviendrait à l'œuvre de M. Oscar Wilde. Pièce, poème, rêverie? ... Elle n'est pas sans valeur. On y rencontre d'heureuses expressions, des énumérations éloquentes et d'assez abondantes trouvailles poétiques: trouvailles ou "rencontres." Le personnage de Salomé, enragé d'amour au point de ne pas voir l'homme qui se tue à côté d'elle et pour elle, est assez bien rendu, dans sa simplicité de bête chaude et frénétique. Celui d'Hérode pareillement. Mais, si je suis à peu près fixé sur l'impression que j'ai ressentie à *Salomé*, je le suis un peu moins sur la valeur proper de l'œuvre. Pour tout dire je ne suis pas bien convaincu que ces énumérations, ces rugissements de bête en rut, et aussi ces "réseumés" philosophiques soient de la bonne poésie. Le poème de M. Wilde n'est pas, assurément, dépourvu de mérite. Il a du mérite; je ne suis pas très sur qu'il ait plus que cela. C'est quelque chose sans doute; mais pas tout à fait assez pour proclamer le "génie" de M. Wilde. Il me paraît plutôt un littérateur adroit qu'un poète inspiré, c'est-à-dire à peu près le contraire de ce qu'on veut nous faire croire ...

[Translation]

The great event of the evening was the performance of Oscar Wilde's *Salomé* ... I was speaking earlier of the artless claim of these exalted and ingenious writers; they are firmly convinced that the production of *Salomé* will hasten the release of the author, imprisoned at the moment for reasons known far and wide. I do not have absolute confidence ... Let us speak of *Salomé*, then, as if we were not responsible for a prisoner's freedom.

I am not sure what name suits the work of Oscar Wilde. Play, poem, dream? ... It is not without value. One encounters in it well-chosen expressions, eloquent recitations and fairly abundant poetic discoveries: discoveries or "encounters." The character of Salomé, madly in love to the point of not noticing the man who kills himself right next to and for her, is all well developed in the simplicity of an ardent and frantic beast. So is the character of Herod. But, if I am more or less settled on my impression of Salomé herself, I am a little less settled on the true value of the work as a whole. To be honest, I am not quite convinced that these recitations, these howls of a beast in heat, and even these philosophical "summaries" are good poetry. Mr. Wilde's poem is not, assuredly, deprived of merit. It has merit; I am not really sure that it has more than that. This is doubtless something; but not quite enough to proclaim the "genius" of Mr. Wilde. He seems to me more a skilled writer than an inspired poet, that is to say, almost the opposite of what one would want us to believe....

11. From Jean de Tinan, "Théâtre de l'oeuvre: *Salomé*" [review of the Paris premiere], *Mercure de France* (March 1896): 415-17 [my translation]

[In contrast to the preceding review, the following notice celebrates the Paris premiere of *Salome*, noting both the quality of the acting and the play's exceptional appeal to emotional and sensory experience.]

M. Lugné-Poe[1] lui-même a composé le personnage d'Hérode avec une souplesse, une exactitude nerveuse d'intonations et d'attitudes, un souci de plastique, qui font, je crois, de ce rôle du Tétrarque le plus parfait de ceux où je l'ai vu. Avoir monté *Salomé* et l'avoir jouée ainsi, c'est s'être attiré la bonne reconnaissance de ceux-là qui aiment cet art de toute leur âme—jusqu'à en être très mal vus dans leurs familles. M. Max Barbier[2] a crié les imprécations de Iokanaan d'une voix superbement sonore, et, grand, a su trouver les gestes qu'il fallait pour paraître gigantesque. Mlle Suzanne Després,[3] page d'Hérodias, s'est trop exquisement lamentée sur la mort du jeune Syrien—*Il était mon frère et plus qu'un frère! ...*—pour que personne ait songé, charmé que l'on était, que c'était le passage dangereux,—il a peut-être tout sauvé, ce petit page, avec sa jolie voix et sa beauté timide—le passage où les amis de la pièce sont tout prêts à interdire à leurs voisins de se moucher. Personne ne s'est mouché, et l'on a acclamé le drame, et l'on a acclamé le nom de M. Oscar Wilde avec tout l'enthousiasme d'admirations qui se multiplient par des indignations; nous souhaitons qu'il parvienne au poète quelque echo de ces acclamations, et que la sincérité de ces sympathies l'encourage dans la terrible épreuve qu'il subit....

[Of the actress portraying Salome, Lina Munte,[4] de Tinan writes the following:]

Cette voix et cette beauté m'ont traîné, dans un vertige, vers d'éblouissant abîmes de luxure d'art et d'amour. Au son de cette voix, au

---

1 Aurélien Marie Lugné (1869-1940), known as Lugné-Poe, was a French actor, director, and set designer whose professional home was the Théâtre de l'Oeuvre.

2 In addition to starring in Paul Claudel's *The Hostage* in 1915 (also staged at the Théâtre de l'Oeuvre), Max Barbier (dates unknown) was the first actor to portray the role of Iokanaan.

3 Suzanne Després (1875-1951) was a French actress married to Lugné-Poe.

4 Caroline Mundt (1854-1909), known on the stage as Lina Munte, was the first actress to perform the role of Salome.

contact de ces gestes, j'ai su que se crispaient en moi des choses de sensualité, de fureur, de tendresse et d'extase que je n'avais pas encore su y trouver. J'ai été oppressé d'attention jusqu'à souffrir.

J'ai été ému jusqu'à avoir la pauvre naïveté de regretter, pour la première fois, de n'avoir pas le génie d'écrire un drame sublime et digne d'elle pour le lui porter—je me suis désolé, et je m'en vante, à penser que je ne connaîtrais pas la joie d'art terrifiante que ce serait d'entendre dire par elle des phrases de soi—de *soi*—et j'ai pensé que n'avoir pas été là, n'avoir pas vu sa *Salomé* plus belle et plus terrible qu'il ne l'avait rêvée, c'était pour Oscar Wilde le plus cruel malheur dont un artiste dût être inconsolable.

[Translation]

Mr. Lugné-Poe himself played the role of Herod with a suppleness, a spirited precision of intonations and mannerisms, a pliable anxiety, which makes, I believe, the role of Tetrarch the most perfect of those I have seen him portray. To have produced *Salomé* and acted in it as well, is to attract the attention of those who love this art with all their soul—even when it risks the disapproval of loved ones. M. Max Barbier cried out the curses of Iokanaan in a superbly sonorous voice and, in the main, knew how to find the gestures necessary to seem prodigious. Miss Suzanne Després, the page of Herodias, only too exquisitely lamented the death of the young Syrian—*He was my brother and more than a brother!* ...—so that no one would have thought, charmed as they were, that this was the dangerous passage—he has perhaps rescued everything, this little page with his little voice and timid beauty—the passage where fans of the play are ready to stop their neighbors from even sniffling. Nobody sniffed, and the drama was acclaimed, and the name of Mr. Oscar Wilde was acclaimed with an enthusiastic praise enhanced by indignation. We wish that some echo of these acclamations would reach the poet, and that the sincerity of these sympathies might encourage him during the terrible trial he suffers....

[...]

This voice [of Lina Munte] and this beauty pulled me into a vertigo, toward dazzling abysses of erotic and aesthetic luxury. Upon hearing this voice and encountering these gestures, I knew that sensuous things arose within me, things of fury, of tenderness and of ecstasy that I had not found there before. I was rapt to the point of suffering.

I was moved to the point of having the wretched simplicity to regret, for the first time, not having had the genius to write a sublime and worthy drama to bring before her. I was saddened, I freely admit, to think that I would not know the joy of terrifying art that it would be to hear her utter lines written by oneself—*oneself*—and I thought that to not have been there, to not have seen his *Salomé* more beautiful and more terrible than he ever dreamed it, was for Oscar Wilde the cruelest misfortune, which must render an artist inconsolable.

12. From "Salome," *The Saturday Review* (13 May 1905): 623-24

[The following excerpt is taken from a review of a performance of *Salome* at the Bijou Theatre in London.]

The mischief, for me, lay in the quality of the acting and of the stage-management; and, deeper, it lay in my conviction that not even the best acting and the best stage-management could make this play so good to see as it is good to read. Of course, I do not mean that "Salome" has less dramatic than literary fibre. Mr. Wilde was a born dramatist—a born theatrist, too. Not less than in his handling of the quick and complex form of modern comedy, there was mastery in his handling of this slow and simple form of tragedy—a form compounded, seemingly, of Sophocles[1] and Maeterlinck in even proportions. The note of terror in "Salome" is struck well in the opening lines, and then slowly the play's action advances, step by step, to the foreknown crisis; and it is mainly through this very slowness, this constant air of suspense, that the play yields us the tragic thrill....

---

1   Ancient Greek tragedian, perhaps best known for *Oedipus the King*, *Electra*, and *Antigone*.

13. Photograph of Alice Guszalewicz in Costume as Salome, c. 1910

[Alice Guszalewicz (1879-1940) performed the title role in Richard Strauss's opera *Salome* in Cologne in 1906. This photograph was for many years misidentified as representing Oscar Wilde himself.]

14. "The Cult of the Clitoris," *The Vigilante* (16 February 1918): 1

[In 1918, Noel Pemberton Billington claimed the existence of a "Black Book" identifying British citizens considered to be sexual deviants and thus vulnerable to being blackmailed by the German government. In this anonymous notice, he accuses Maud Allan, the dancer famous for her "Vision of Salome," of being one of those named (see Introduction, pp. 34-35).]

To be a member of Maud Allan's private performances in Oscar Wilde's "Salome," one has to apply to a Miss Valetta, of 9, Duke Street, Adelphi W.C. If Scotland Yard were to seize the list of these members I have no doubt they would secure the names of several of the first 47,000.

15. From the Verbatim Report of the Trial of Noel Pemberton Billington, MP, on a Charge of Criminal Libel (London: Vigilante Office, 1918), 95, 97, 100, 286

[In response to Billington's accusation, Maud Allan sued him for libel. During the trial, Billington, who undertook his own defense, repeatedly assailed Allan's character by insisting that *Salome* was itself an immoral play. Allan's defense of the play is striking (see Introduction, pp. 34-35).]

BILLINGTON: Are you quite aware of what Mr. Oscar Wilde has written here?

ALLAN: I am only aware of how I read the lines.

BILLINGTON: Do you notice the particular stress which the author puts on the Moon during the whole of this play?

ALLAN: Yes.

BILLINGTON: Has that any particular significance that you know of?

ALLAN: It shows how the Moon appeared to several of the characters in it.

BILLINGTON: Have you read any of the other works of Mr. Oscar Wilde?

ALLAN: Yes.

BILLINGTON: Do you appreciate that he is a great artist?

ALLAN: I think him a great artist.

BILLINGTON: Never likely to employ words unless they had a direct meaning, every word he uses, being an artist, has a direct meaning?

ALLAN: Artists paint, you know.

BILLINGTON: Will you answer?

ALLAN: I am answering.

BILLINGTON: He is not a man likely to use words which have no meaning?

ALLAN: I do not know him other than in his works. I can only judge from what I have read.

BILLINGTON: In studying Art did you endeavour to so study it as that you could give a faithful representation of what was going on in the author's mind when he wrote the work?

ALLAN: That is a very problematical thing. One never can know exactly what happens in the author's mind, one can only see the words and read them as you feel you can read them and interpret them, the same in music, no two people interpret exactly alike.

[...]

BILLINGTON: She [Salome] says "The moon is cold and chaste"? (p. 53)

ALLAN: Yes, and good to see. "She is like a little piece of money, you would think she was a little silver flower. The moon is cold and chaste. I am sure she is a virgin, she has a virgin's beauty. Yes, she is a virgin. She has never defiled herself. She has never abandoned herself to men, like the other goddesses." (p. 53)

BILLINGTON: Salome is likening herself to the moon?

ALLAN: Not at all ... she never mentions herself at all there, she only means that she admires what is beautiful and how she hates everything that is coarse and vulgar.

[...]

BILLINGTON: You say that it is not the first time a woman has asked to kiss a man's mouth, perhaps you are right, but would it be a physical or a spiritual performance?

ALLAN: I could tell you what we think but what you would not think.

DARLING: But you could tell us what is your idea?

ALLAN: I consider that Salome here is a child who loves the beautiful, who sees in this man something quite different from what she has seen round about her, because when she enters from the banqueting hall she tells how she loathes the spilling wine and the uncouth man takes possession of her, and she finds in this man, in his body, everything that is beautiful.

[...]

[Billington also brought to the stand Lord Alfred Douglas himself to discuss Wilde's original intentions in writing *Salome*. It is important to keep in mind that Wilde and Douglas argued vociferously over the translation of *Salome*, rendering his account an illuminating, if unreliable one. His interpretation of the play is decidedly different from that of Allan.]

LORD ALFRED DOUGLAS: I have never seen the play acted. But, of course, I translated the play from the French, and I had many conversations with Wilde about it, and I have a very particular knowledge of what he meant by the play because, as the translator, I had to know exactly what he was driving at. I heard him discuss it not only before the translation but on innumerable occasions with other people, with French men of letters, and so on afterwards in Paris, so I have a very particular knowledge of what his intentions were in writing the play.

MR. JUSTICE DARLING: Will you tell us what his intentions, as expressed to you, were?

DOUGLAS: I can say that he intended the play to be an exhibition of perverted sexual passion excited in a young girl; and there are other things in it. I am only dealing with the particular subjects which have arisen in this case, and there is one passage which is sodomitic which is meant to be sodomitic.

DARLING: He told you that?

DOUGLAS: Yes. He did not use the word "sodomitic." Wilde was a man who cloaked up those things in flowery language. He never used the word "sodomitic." He would express horror at such language. Anything like the "Cult of the Clitoris" would fill him with as much horror as it apparently does Mr Hume-Williams.[1]

---

1   Ellis Hume-Williams (1863-1947) was Maud Allan's prosecutor in the case, along with Travers Humphreys (1867-1956), who notably served as Junior Counsel in Wilde's libel action against Queensberry.

Select Bibliography

Baum, Rob K. "*Salomé*: Re/Dressing Wilde on the Rim." *The Victorian Comic Spirit: New Perspectives*. Ed. Jennifer Wagner-Lawlor. Aldershot, UK: Ashgate, 2000. 205-18.

Becker-Leckrone, Megan. "*Salome*: The Fetishization of a Textual Corpus." *New Literary History* 26.2 (Spring 1995): 239-60.

Bennett, Chad. "Oscar Wilde's *Salome*: Décor, Des Corps, Desire." *ELH* 77.2 (Summer 2010): 297-324.

Bennett, Michael Y., ed. *Refiguring Oscar Wilde's* Salome. New York: Rodopi, 2011.

Bigliazzi, Silvia. "Collaborating Media and Symbolic Fractures in Wilde's *Salome*." *Collaboration in the Arts from the Middle Ages to the Present*. Ed. Silvia Bigliazzi and Sharon Wood. Burlington, VT: Ashgate, 2006. 79-90.

Burns, Edward. "*Salomé*: Wilde's Radical Tragedy." *Rediscovering Oscar Wilde*. Ed. C. George Sandulescu. Gerrards Cross, UK: Colin Smythe, 1994. 30-36.

Davis, W. Eugene. "Oscar Wilde, *Salome*, and the German Press 1902-1905." *English Literature in Transition (1880-1920)* 44.2 (2001): 149-80.

Dellamora, Richard. "Traversing the Feminine in Oscar Wilde's *Salomé*." *Victorian Sages and Cultural Discourse: Renegotiating Gender and Power*. Ed. Thais E. Morgan. New Brunswick, NJ: Rutgers UP, 1990. 246-64.

Dierkes-Thrun, Petra. "'The Brutal Music and the Delicate Text'? The Aesthetic Relationship between Wilde's and Strauss's *Salome* Reconsidered." *Modern Language Quarterly* 69.3 (Sept. 2008): 367-89.

——. "Salomé, C'est Moi? Salome and Wilde as Icons of Sexual Transgression." *Approaches to Teaching the Works of Oscar Wilde*. Ed. Philip E. Smith, II. New York: Modern Language Association of America, 2008. 171-79.

Donohue, Joseph. "Distance, Death and Desire in *Salome*." *The Cambridge Companion to Oscar Wilde*. Ed. Peter Raby. Cambridge: Cambridge UP, 1997. 118-42.

Downey, Katherine Brown. *Perverse Midrash: Oscar Wilde, André Gide, and Censorship of Biblical Drama*. New York: Continuum, 2004.

Fernbach, Amanda. "Wilde's *Salomé* and the Ambiguous Fetish." *Victorian Literature and Culture* 29.1 (2001): 195-218.

Garland, Tony. "Deviant Desires and Dance: The *Femme Fatale*

Status of Salome and the Dance of the Seven Veils." Michael
Bennett, 125-44.

Gilbert, Elliot L. "'Tumult of Images': Wilde, Beardsley, and
Salomé." *Victorian Studies* 26.2 (Winter 1983): 133-59.

Gladden, Samuel Lyndon. "Unveiling *Salomé*: The Word-Made-Flesh
Undone." *Approaches to Teaching the Works of Oscar Wilde.* Ed.
Philip E. Smith, II. New York: Modern Language Association of
America, 2008. 180-87.

Harris, Frank. *Oscar Wilde: His Life and Confessions.* New York:
Brentano's, 1918.

Hartwig, Heidi. "Dancing for an Oath: *Salomé*'s Revaluation of Word
and Gesture." *Modern Drama* 45.1 (Spring 2002): 23-34.

Hofer, Matthew, ed. *Oscar Wilde in America: The Interviews.* Champaign: U of Illinois P, 2013.

Hutcheon, Linda, and Hutcheon, Michael. "'Here's Lookin' at You,
Kid': The Empowering Gaze in *Salomé.*" *Profession* (1998): 11-22.

Kellogg-Dennis, Patricia. "Oscar Wilde's *Salomé*: Symbolist
Princess." *Rediscovering Oscar Wilde.* Ed. C. George Sandulescu.
Gerrards Cross, UK: Colin Smythe, 1994. 224-31.

Lawler, Donald. "The Gothic Wilde." *Rediscovering Oscar Wilde.* Ed.
C. George Sandulescu. Gerrards Cross, UK: Smythe, 1994. 249-68.

Lewsadder, Matthew. "Removing the Veils: Censorship, Female Sexuality, and Oscar Wilde's *Salome.*" *Modern Drama* 45.4 (Winter
2002): 519-44.

Macdonald, Ian Andrew. "Oscar Wilde as a French Writer: Considering Wilde's French in *Salomé.*" Michael Bennett 1-20.

Marcovitch, Heather. "The Princess, Persona, and Subjective Desire:
A Reading of Oscar Wilde's *Salome.*" *Papers on Language and Literature* 40.1 (Winter 2004): 88-101.

Marcus, Sharon. "*Salomé*!! Sarah Bernhardt, Oscar Wilde, and the
Drama of Celebrity." *PMLA: Publications of the Modern Language
Association of America* 126.4 (October 2011): 999-1021, 1187-88.

Mason, Stuart [Christopher Millard]. *Bibliography of Oscar Wilde.*
London: Bertram Rota, 1967.

Mitchell, Jason P. "A Source Victorian or Biblical?: The Integration
of Biblical Diction and Symbolism in Oscar Wilde's *Salomé.*" *Victorian Newsletter* 89 (Spring 1996): 14-18.

——. "*Salome* and the Wildean Art of Symbolist Theatre." *Modern
Drama* 37 (Spring 1994): 104-19.

——. "Translator's Preface." *Salome.* Trans. Joseph Donohue. Charlottesville: U of Virginia P, 2011. vii-xxviii.

Nassaar, Christopher S. "Pater's *The Renaissance* and Wilde's
Salomé." *Explicator* 59.2 (Winter 2001): 80-82.

———. "Wilde's *Salomé* and the Victorian Religious Landscape." *Wildean: The Journal of the Oscar Wilde Society* 20 (January 2002): 2-13.

Navarre, Joan. "Oscar Wilde and the Motif of Looking: An Approach to Teaching Gender Issues in *Salomé.*" *Approaches to Teaching the Works of Oscar Wilde.* Ed. Philip E. Smith, II. New York: Modern Language Association of America, 2008. 157-62.

———. "Paul Verlaine and A Platonic Lament: Beardsley's Portrayal of a Parallel Love Story in Wilde's *Salome.*" *English Literature in Transition 1880-1920* 51.2 (2008): 152-63.

Powell, Kerry. "*Salomé*, the Censor, and the Divine Sarah." *Oscar Wilde and the Theatre of the 1890s.* Cambridge: Cambridge UP, 1990. 33-54.

Praz, Mario. "*Salome* in Literary Tradition." *Richard Strauss: Salome.* Ed. Derrick Puffett. Cambridge: Cambridge UP, 1989.

Pyle, Forest. "Extravagance; or, Salomé's Kiss." *Journal of Pre-Raphaelite Studies* 7 (Fall 1998): 39-52.

Quigley, Austin E. "Realism and Symbolism in Oscar Wilde's *Salomé.*" *Modern Drama* 37 (Spring 1994): 104-19.

Richmond-Garza, Elizabeth. "The Double Life of *Salomé*: Sexuality, Nationalism and Self-Translation in Oscar Wilde." Michael Bennett, 21-36.

Rix, Robert. "*Salomé* and the fin du globe: Oscar Wilde's Decadent Tragedy." *Fin de Siècle / New Beginnings.* Ed. Ib Johansen. Aarhus, Denmark: Aarhus UP, 2000. 94-124.

Robinson, Bonnie J. Robinson. "The Perversion of Decadence: The Cases of Oscar Wilde's *Dorian Gray* and *Salome.*" *Decadences: Morality and Aesthetics in British Literature.* Ed. Paul Fox. Stuttgart, Germany: Ibidem, 2006. 147-67.

Rose, Marilyn Gaddis. "The Synchronic *Salome.*" *The Languages of Theatre: Problems in the Translation and Transposition of Drama.* Ed. Otrun Zuber. Elmsford, NY: Pergamon, 1980. 146-52.

Russ, Andrew R. "Wilde's *Salome*: The Chastity, Promiscuity and Monstrosity of Symbols." Michael Bennett 37-54.

Salamensky, S.I. "Wilde Women: *Salomé* and the Spectacle of the Transgendered Jewess Hysteric." *The Modern Art of Influence and the Spectacle of Oscar Wilde.* New York: Palgrave Macmillan, 2012. 35-72.

Salbayre, Sébastien. "Biblical Turns of Phrase, Repetition and Circularity in Oscar Wilde's *Salome.*" *Cahiers Victoriens et Edouardiens* 63 (April 2006): 175-86.

Schweik, Robert C. "Oscar Wilde's *Salomé*, the Salome Theme in Late European Art, and a Problem of Method in Cultural History." Ed. O.M. Brack. *Twilight of Dawn.* Tucson: U of Arizona P, 1987.

Shannon, Beth Tashery. "Viewing *Salomé* Symbolically." *Approaches to Teaching the Works of Oscar Wilde*. Ed. Philip E. Smith, II. New York: Modern Language Association of America, 2008. 163-70.

Skaggs, Carmen Trammell. "Modernity's Revision of the Dancing Daughter: The Salome Narrative of Wilde and Strauss." *College Literature* 29.3 (Summer 2002): 124-39.

Snodgrass, Chris. "Wilde's *Salome*: Turning 'the Monstrous Beast' into a Tragic Hero." *Oscar Wilde: The Man, His Writings, and His World*. Ed. Robert N. Keane. New York: AMS, 2003. 183-96.

Stokes, John. *Oscar Wilde: Myths, Miracles, and Imitations*. Cambridge: Cambridge UP, 1996.

Tabak, Jennie. "Medusa Is No Longer Laughing: Oscar Wilde's Symbolism in *Salomé*." *Journal of Theatre and Drama* 7-8 (2001-02): 159-73.

Toepfer, Karl. "The Voice of Rapture: A Symbolist System of Ecstatic Speech in Oscar Wilde's *Salomé*." *American University Studies* XXVI: Theater Arts 7. New York: Peter Lang, 1991.

Townsend, Julie. "Staking *Salomé*: The Literary Forefathers and Choreographic Daughters of Oscar Wilde's 'Hysterical and Perverted Creature.'" *Oscar Wilde and Modern Culture: The Making of a Legend*. Ed. Joseph Bristow. Athens: Ohio UP, 2008. 154-79.

Tydeman, William and Steven Price. *Wilde: Salome*. Cambridge: Cambridge UP, 1996.

Wallerstein, Nicholas. "Classical and Religious Rhetoric in Oscar Wilde's *Salomé*." *Language and Literature* 23 (1998): 61-72.

Wilde, Oscar. *Salome*. Trans. Lord Alfred Douglas. New York: Dover Publications, 1967.

——. *Salome*. Trans. Vyvyan Holland. London: Folio Press, 1974.

——. *Salome*. Trans. Robert Ross. *Collected Works of Oscar Wilde*. London: Wordsworth, 2007. 717-42.

——. *Salome*. Trans. Richard Ellmann. *Major Works*. New York: Oxford UP, 2008. 299-330.

——. *Salome*. Trans. Joseph Donohue. Charlottesville: U of Virginia P, 2011.

from the publisher

A name never says it all, but the word "broadview" expresses a good deal of the philosophy behind our company. We are open to a broad range of academic approaches and political viewpoints. We pay attention to the broad impact book publishing and book printing has in the wider world; we began using recycled stock more than a decade ago, and for some years now we have used 100% recycled paper for most titles. As a Canadian-based company we naturally publish a number of titles with a Canadian emphasis, but our publishing program overall is internationally oriented and broad-ranging. Our individual titles often appeal to a broad readership too; many are of interest as much to general readers as to academics and students.

Founded in 1985, Broadview remains a fully independent company owned by its shareholders—not an imprint or subsidiary of a larger multinational.

If you would like to find out more about Broadview and about the books we publish, please visit us at **www.broadviewpress.com**. And if you'd like to place an order through the site, we'd like to show our appreciation by extending a special discount to you: by entering the code below you will receive a 20% discount on purchases made through the Broadview website.

Discount code: **broadview20%**

Thank you for choosing Broadview.

Please note: this offer applies only to sales of bound books within the United States or Canada.

The interior of this book is printed on 100% recycled paper.